For Sheila,
for Love and for Life

Acknowledgments

My love, my thanks to the Third Street Writers Group: Montserrat Fontes, Janet Gregory, Jeffrey N. McMahan, Karen Sandler, Gerald Citrin—good friends, respected colleagues, wonderfully ruthless critics of all my work during all our years together.

In memoriam, Naomi Sloan...deeply cherished and missed by us all.

To "Jason," for technical advice offered with patience and humor... Her professionalism and dedication are incorporated facets of this novel; she has greatly expanded my insights into her difficult profession.

To Detective Supervisor Mary F. Otterson, Madison, Wis., who has also added immeasurably to my respect for women in police work; her friendship and uncommon generosity continue to deepen my understanding of Kate Delafield.

– 1 –

Turning off Burton Way onto Arnaz Drive, Detective Kate Delafield drifted the Plymouth across Colgate Avenue and through the single lane allowed by half a dozen double-parked black-and-whites, their light bars pulsing brilliantly in the darkness. Ed Taylor, her partner, had arrived; his Caprice was squeezed head-in between two TV network vans. She drove past a glare of television camera lights, past dozens of spectators herded behind barricades and police tape, past a sign at the end of Arnaz Drive:

BEVERLY HILLS CITY LIMIT
OVERNIGHT PARKING PROHIBITED

She parked around the corner on Clifton Way, the southern dividing line between the Division's northernmost, westernmost reporting District 701 and the city of Beverly Hills. She had never been called to investigate a death anywhere near this upscale section of Wilshire Division.

Shoving her hands into the pockets of her gray windbreaker, she walked briskly toward the cacophony of squawking police radios, glancing around her at the solid row of shadowed two- and three-story apartment buildings lining both sides of the street. She wore a white crewneck sweater under the windbreaker, and black corduroy pants and Nike shoes — inappropriate garb; but she had not been home to change clothes when her beeper summoned her to the telephone and then here to Arnaz Drive.

She paused amid the crowd gathered around Lieutenant Bodwin, who stood bathed in brilliant light as a KTTV reporter, a young woman vaguely familiar to Kate, interviewed him. Nearby, other TV and radio station personnel jostled for position, for their own turn at Bodwin.

". . . preliminary stages," Bodwin was saying in low tones, his craggy face solemn. "We have no further information at this time."

A gang-shooting on the eastside, Kate reflected dourly, would receive a mere mention on the news — but a homicide this close to Rodeo Drive was bound to draw a circus train of media coverage.

Turning her back on the spectacle, she examined the locale of this crime scene, a two-story beige stucco with large, splashy gold script across its front: *The Beverly Malibu.* The entrance and upper front apartment windows were framed in bright turquoise mosaic tile flecked with gold, the only foliage two thick clusters of bird-of-paradise flanking the entry-way.

This building was an anomaly on the block, in garish discord with its newer, more elegant neighbors. It filled its modest allotment of land, narrow paths along each side closed off by padlocked wooden gates. Six parking spaces under the building's front overhang, not nearly sufficient for the building's inhabitants, confirmed that the Beverly Malibu had been constructed decades ago, before L.A. apartment building codes mandated self-contained parking.

Kate pulled her notebook from her shoulder bag and recorded the time, 7:23 pm, and the date, November 24, 1988, and her first note: only three tenant cars parked under the building. Then she attached her badge to her jacket and ducked under the yellow police tape.

Sergeant Fred Hansen, stolidly watching Lieutenant Bodwin and the two patrol officers assigned to crowd control, guarded the entryway, his feet spread, one hand holding a clipboard, the other resting above his holster. He spotted Kate and nodded, his somber gaze taking in her apparel.

He gestured toward the television lights, his bland features hardening. "The landlady called some of these media people. She's got a very big mouth."

She shrugged. "What's the story here, Fred?"

He consulted his clipboard. "Victim is Owen Sinclair, seventy-three, retired. Some kind of movie director in the old days, the landlady says. We logged

3

the call at six-oh-four." He glanced up at her. "He died real hard, Kate. From the looks of him . . ." He shook his head. "Ed's waiting upstairs, rear apartment."

Unless Hansen had some insight to offer — and he rarely did — she needed no further details; she would see for herself soon enough. She gestured with her head toward the building. "Your officers canvassing?"

He nodded. "There's fourteen tenants besides Sinclair, only nine here right now. That's all I've got so far."

"Thanks, Fred," she said in mechanical acknowledgement of the bare bones report. She walked up the path past the dust-coated bird-of-paradise and entered the Beverly Malibu.

The lobby, its floor of gray tile, was no larger than a walk-in closet. Mail boxes lined one wall. Kate glanced at the boxes, scanning names without absorbing them. One name was accompanied by the bold statement MANAGER. Fifteen apartments singly occupied by fifteen residents . . .

To the left of the lobby an arched doorway led to a room with green indoor-outdoor carpeting, a sink and a formica-covered counter, a long table and folding chairs, a television set. On the counter evidence remained of a gathering earlier in the day: a punch bowl and a disorder of plastic glasses, paper plates, napkins, utensils. Odd, Kate thought, for so old and relatively small a building to offer a community room.

She glanced down the hallway. Two officers she could not see clearly enough to identify stood in a doorway talking to a tenant. She counted five doors

4

on the left, four on the right, including the manager's. Obviously these apartments were singles and/or one bedroom. The remaining six upstairs must be two-bedroom. She climbed worn gray carpeted stairs to the second floor.

She nodded to Knapp, who stood guarding the hallway; Hollings, his partner, was undoubtedly in one of the apartments gathering information. Taylor, in brown pants and a brown plaid jacket over a yellow polo shirt, his arms crossed above his paunch, lounged against the wall at the end of the hall. He waved his notebook in greeting and walked toward her.

"So happy Thanksgiving," he growled.

She asked sympathetically, "Did you at least get dinner with the family?"

"Yeah, Bert and his wife got in from Oceanside about twelve, we ate mid-afternoon." Taylor's face had softened at the mention of his oldest son. He glanced at her clothing. "How about you, Kate? Out visiting, right?"

She nodded. "Munched on a turkey leg on the way here." It was literally true. She had been with Maggie Schaeffer and some friends at Maggie's house in the Valley; they had planned to go to the Nightwood Bar after dinner.

"The sonofabitch that spoiled your dinner —" Taylor jerked with his thumb, "I guarantee somebody sure spoiled his."

Kate peered past the open door of apartment 13, at a chaos of stereo equipment overwhelming the living room — record players, tape decks, compact disc players, speakers large and small — all piled on cabinets or scattered over the worn shag carpeting.

Two speakers hung from the walls, above long shelves stuffed with records and tapes. The apartment was imbued with the faint but settled odor of cigar smoke.

Taylor stepped into the living room. "The other bedroom's nothing but floor-to-ceiling records, lots of the old forty-fives and seventy-eights."

Kate glanced at a sofa covered with a fringed cotton throw, at cheap blond tables and nondescript lamps, a worn leather recliner. Taylor strode down the hallway. Kate followed, scowling at the heavy tread of his feet, envisioning delicate strands of evidence crushed to obliteration under those big leather soles.

Three rooms opened off the hallway — one with the recordings Taylor had mentioned, another a bathroom, and finally the murder scene. Taylor stepped aside, to allow her entry.

Owen Sinclair's boxer shorts-clad body lay on its side, facing her. He was arched severely and rigidly backward, his legs straight out behind him. There were claw marks across his stomach from his own fingernails; the nails on the hand stretched toward her were caked with blood. The other arm was handcuffed to a bar of the brass headboard. The purple face was ratcheted into a sardonic leer, the eyeballs a solid red hemorrhage.

"His eyes," Taylor said. "That's what I call a hangover."

Wondering what unfortunate had first come upon this room of death, she asked, "Who found him?"

Taylor consulted his notebook. "Paula Grant and her niece, Aimee Grant, who's visiting her. The apartment next door. Ms. Grant and the niece were on their way out for dinner. Our handsome corpse took their appetite clean away."

Feeling Owen Sinclair's blood-pool eyes on her, she made her way carefully around the chair beside the bed.

The bedclothes had been ravaged by Owen Sinclair's death throes, the thermal blanket and top sheet a tangled mess, the bottom sheet ripped from the scourings of his feet.

"S and M," Taylor suggested, pointing to the handcuffs. "Then he OD'd on some fancy new drug."

"We've never seen an OD look like him," she countered. "But anything's possible." Carefully, she moved closer to him.

The sagging, hirsute skin surfaces were mottled faintly purple, but Sinclair's arms were free of needle marks. She touched his shoulder. Surprised, she pulled her hand away. "He's not even nearly cold. But look at him, Ed — complete rigor."

"Yeah, I never saw it this quick either." Taylor had turned his attention to the night table beside the bed. It held a compact disc player, a jumble of glasses and cups, some of them containing dregs, a key which Kate recognized as belonging to the handcuffs, and a telephone, its cord visibly cut.

"This chair . . ." Kate was looking at the cheap metal chair beside the bed, its seat and back of red plastic.

"Yeah, I already checked it out. It's from the kitchen." Taylor scratched his thin blond hair, then pulled the strands back into place. "I figure this, Kate. Somebody hooked him up to his bed for some S and M jollies. Then gave him something, cut the phone, got this chair, sat down here and just

7

watched. I'm betting we got a sicko on our hands — somebody that thinks it's party time to torture somebody, watch them take a long time to croak."

Kate said quietly, "Right now I can't really argue with that scenario."

"The chair's a good possible for prints."

Looking at the night table, she nodded. The handcuff key was too ridged for a print. "The phone, too. If we're dealing with the sicko you describe, our killer may have picked it up to show the victim the cut cord. To taunt him."

"I say we superglue the chair and phone."

As the D-3 on this homicide team, she had immediate jurisdiction over the crime scene and could order investigatory processes she deemed necessary. Conventional fingerprint dusting usually produced workable results. Superglue, sprayed as an adhesive mist and then stained to illuminate all fingerprints, was a sophisticated but costly process: it rendered most objects it coated virtually unusable. But she ordered it when necessary, just as she had in other instances commanded chunks of carpeting to be excised for bloodstain testing, rooms dismantled in a search for weapons or other evidence. She was a sanctioned intruder, empowered to search unhindered through private lives.

"Right," she said, scrutinizing the metal and plastic components of the chair. Perhaps superglue could isolate a high resolution print.

She turned away from the bed to examine the rest of the room: a simple dresser, no mirror; a portable television on a stand; two cardboard cartons, one neatly filled with sports magazines, the other with well-used paperbacks, their covers cracked and torn.

At the end of the bed were the clothes Owen Sinclair had dropped: cotton pants, a print sport shirt, canvas loafers.

Kate moved over to the dresser and surveyed a half-dozen or so bottles of men's toiletries, all unopened, suggesting they were gifts; a well-used set of old-fashioned silver-backed brushes monogrammed OCS; a set of keys; a gold Seiko watch; a few coins scattered beside a worn leather wallet. There were also two framed five-by-seven photos on the dresser, and numerous others clustered above it along the wall.

Using her pen, she flipped open the wallet. Aged yellow plastic blurred the identifying photo on a driver's license, but she could read the name, Owen Charles Sinclair, and the date of birth, 10-12-1915. Visible were the edges of a wad of bills in the folding money compartment.

She glanced back at the victim. A braided gold chain lay in muted glitter amid the tufted chest hair; the clawed hand cuffed to the bed bore an emerald ring with a heavy gold setting. Apparently robbery had played no part in this homicide, adding further credibility to Taylor's scenario.

In one of the photos on the dresser, a faded black and white snapshot, a man in his early thirties, wearing crisply pressed pants and a Hawaiian shirt with a scarf at the neck, leaned against a fifties-vintage car, his arms crossed over his thick chest. The smiling face was floridly handsome, the hair unusually thick and wavy. Kate glanced from the photo to the figure on the bed and then back. The victim's blooded eyes and leering face hindered comparison, but the body type was similar and there was no mistaking the Cesar Romero shock of wavy gray hair.

The second photo was in color, of a brown-haired young man in army camouflage fatigues, two ammunition belts over his slender shoulders, a canteen hanging from his waist. Rifle in hand, a muddied boot on the fender of a mud-splattered jeep, he grinned over his shoulder at the camera. Kate peered closely at the weapon: an M-16. She had seen many such weapons and many such young men during one singular year of her life at Tan Son Nhut air base and Da Nang. Perhaps this fresh-faced, cocksure young grunt was the victim's son — if not a victim himself, one of the fifty thousand American dead in Vietnam.

She looked at the first of the black and white photos on the wall. Six men and two women, most of them in western costume, grinned casually at the camera, their backdrop a saloon — obviously a movie or stage set. Sinclair, his arms draped around the two women, was in the front row, again identifiable by his hair as well as his contemporary shirt and pants.

There were at least two dozen other such group pictures, the cast of faces changing from photo to photo, Owen Sinclair the only constant. She occasionally focused on a vaguely familiar face, an actor or actress she could not place. Hansen, she remembered, had mentioned that Sinclair was once a movie director. B-movies, apparently, featuring character actors whom stardom had forever eluded.

Separate from this collection were a group of portrait photos autographed with the usual platitudes: *All the best. To a great guy,* and signed with first names. Two photos had full signatures, one of them

10

Jack Warner and addressed *To a fine American.* She looked with interest at the balding man with hooded eyes and pencil moustache. In the photo next to Jack Warner, a double-chinned, grandfatherly figure with a fringe of whitish hair, his dark suit pinstriped, shook hands with an equally dark-suited Owen Sinclair. The photograph was simply signed, *J. Parnell Thomas.*

Kate wrote the name in her notebook. If this collection of photos symbolized the achievements of Sinclair's working lifetime, why had it not been given a place of honor in the living room? Why was it hidden back here where viewing would be by invitation only?

She turned to Taylor, who stood with his back to the corpse, watching her, his hands stuffed in his jacket pockets — good procedure to prevent inadvertent touching of any object, but for him, she knew, merely habit.

The technicians arrived — Baker, the fingerprint man, and Shapiro, the photographer; Pete Johnson sketched the murder scene. The coroner would be on the scene shortly. Leaving Taylor to discuss with Baker the fingerprinting technology to be used on this crime scene, Kate walked out of Owen Sinclair's apartment to map the locale. Police presence on the second floor had increased; Foster and Deems escorted a middle-aged woman pale with shock into the apartment across and down from Sinclair's; the patrol officers went into the apartment to gather preliminary information from her.

A fire door next to Sinclair's had no locking mechanism, and Kate carefully pushed it open from the bottom with pressure from her foot. After she walked through the doorway, she held the door by its edges and propped it open with the pocket flashlight in her shoulder bag. She moved slowly down the stairway, studying the stairs and walls. The flight-and-a-half of closed stairs ended in a basement below the first-floor apartments, at an open laundry room with coin washers and dryers. A narrow corridor with a ceiling of plaster-coated pipes led to the front of the building. The door beside her seemed to be a security door locking from the outside, but she did not open it to verify; she would have Baker fingerprint it and all the doors along the stairway, and as soon as possible, before either a tenant or a police officer inadvertently spoiled the possibility for prints — if they had not already done so. She went into the laundry room and looked through its barred window. The back of the Beverly Malibu, illuminated by a dim orange bulb over the rear door, faced a high redwood fence covered with ivy. A narrow path separated the building from the fence.

She recorded this additional access to the building in her notebook, and then walked briskly down the narrow corridor under its ceiling of pipes to the front of the building. She looked again at the mailboxes in the lobby, recording the names of second floor apartments ten through fifteen: D. Kincaid; L. Rothberg; M. Marlowe; C. Crane; and P. Grant, the woman who had discovered the body. The distraught-looking woman Foster and Deems had escorted into apartment 11 was presumably L. Rothberg. Sinclair had occupied apartment 13.

Everson, the deputy coroner, came in the front door, medical bag in hand. He said by way of greeting, "What's a nice girl like you doing in a place like this?"

Grinning, she beckoned him to follow her upstairs.

In Owen Sinclair's apartment Everson snapped on a pair of surgical gloves, then tidily folded his arms and waited, watching the strobe flashes of Shapiro's camera crisscross the corpse of Owen Sinclair.

"Finished here," Shapiro told Kate. "I suppose you want the usual — photos of every square inch of the whole apartment."

The bearded photographer did not smile, nor did Kate. She would acknowledge neither humor nor fault in the thoroughness of her methods, however aggravating they might be. "The usual will be fine," she said evenly. She gestured to the wall of photos. "I'd like individual shots of each of those."

Shapiro shrugged and turned his attention to the wall. Everson, who had been grinning throughout this exchange, reached into his medical bag for a scalpel and then walked over to the bed.

"This won't hurt a bit," he cheerfully told the corpse, and made an incision in the upper right of Sinclair's stomach and plunged a thermometer into what Kate knew was the liver.

He turned to Kate and Taylor and said in a tone of distinct pleasure, "Sometimes medical science is just as exact and pretty as mathematics. Your boy here, he had a dose of strychnine along with his Thanksgiving turkey."

Taylor, writing in his notebook, said, "How do you spell that?"

"T-u-r-k-e-y," said Everson.

"How can you tell, Walt?" Kate asked Everson.

He faced the corpse and recited, "Tetanic bending of the back, sardonic grin, staring eyes, cyanosis of the skin from extreme rise in blood pressure, instant

13

rigor — it's classic. I looked at a corpse exactly like him in med school."

"Poison victims I've seen," Kate mused, "were mostly suicides. And there was vomit and . . ." She shut out the images, her memory of the smells.

Everson nodded. "Sometimes with strychnine too. But not always. It targets the nervous system — spinal cord and brain." He gestured to the rigidly arched, staring corpse. "Severe convulsions — a series of simultaneous muscle contractions, so violent he even broke open the blood vessels in his eyes."

Everson reached for the wrist handcuffed to the bed. "Odds are he broke it during a seizure." He explored the wrist with his long slender fingers. "Indeed he did. Actual cause of death is respiratory failure, Kate. He choked to death from the intensity of his contractions."

Everson withdrew his thermometer, briskly swabbed it clean with cotton, held it up to his eyes. "Two hours ago," he said. He glanced at his chain bracelet watch. "Time of death no earlier than five-thirty."

Kate focused on the kitchen chair beside the bed. She asked quietly, "How long, would you say, to die?"

Everson shrugged. "Depends on a lot of factors, like dosage. A fatal dose begins at maybe ten or fifteen grams. First symptoms appear from fifteen minutes all the way up to an hour, depending on how he ingested it. And he's a big man, large body weight. First he'd feel his chest tighten, he'd start shaking . . . How long to expiration? Ballpark guess is one to three hours after the first symptoms, but I heard of one case where it took more like ten hours."

"Some fun, the poor bastard," muttered Taylor.

Everson shook his head. "Unless this place is soundproof, I'd think someone would hear him. Victims of strychnine don't lose consciousness except momentarily — panic is a major contributor to death. The process is so agonizing, I can't imagine anyone doing it quietly."

The woman across the hall, Kate remembered, had just arrived home. But what about the two women who had discovered the body? Presumably they had been in the apartment adjoining this one while Owen Sinclair was dying . . .

Taylor asked, "Where'd the poison come from, Walt? What's it like?"

"Organic. Used for pest control mostly, I believe. An alkaloid. Exceptionally bitter taste."

Kate looked with increased interest at the empty glasses and cups on the bedside table.

Taylor's gaze was fixed on the same table. "Better bag the glasses," he said.

"Definitely." She would have them all taken to the lab for laser printing and toxicology. "Let's seal off that community room downstairs, too. Maybe the food from that get-together earlier today was involved. We'll just have to see what we find out and how quickly we can find it out."

Everson pulled his tape recorder from the bag. "I assume you two have suspects to browbeat? I have a report to dictate and I'd like to get back to home and hearth sometime tonight."

Kate said to Taylor, "Let's talk to Paula Grant and her niece."

– 2 –

The dark-haired young woman who answered the door of Apartment 14 wore black pants and a white silk shirt figured with silver thread. She stared at the identification Kate extended as if deaf to Kate's introduction of herself and Taylor. Slowly she lifted her gaze to Kate's face.

The eyes were an intense gathering of blue-violet, and looked almost bruised, as if the blue would seep onto her smooth, unmadeup cheekbones. She was young — in her twenties, Kate estimated. And striking in holiday attire that she seemed no more aware of than if she wore a bathrobe.

The blue gaze acquired focus as the young woman took in Kate's face. "Come in." Her voice was low and soft, almost breathless.

A white-haired, exceedingly slender woman moved gracefully across the gray carpet toward them. She wore a cream-colored silk shirt tucked into loosely cut beige trousers, and brown loafers with tassels. "I'm Paula Grant. This is my niece, Aimee Grant." The shoulders were straight, the bearing imperious, the vocal quality Lauren Bacall.

Kate again extended her identification. "I'm Detective Delafield, this is my partner, Detective Taylor. I'm sorry these circumstances bring us together."

Paula Grant's clear hazel eyes ignored Kate's ID to sweep over her windbreaker and corduroy pants.

Out of a sudden, insupportable sense of deficiency, Kate said, "I was away visiting when I was called here," even as she realized that she had never before done such a thing in her professional life. She felt Taylor's stare.

"Of course," said Paula Grant. "Please sit down."

But Kate knew that she was diminished in the eyes of this aristocratic woman. One simply should not dress this way wherever one might be on Thanksgiving Day.

She said to Paula Grant, "We need to ask you and your niece some questions, and we'll need to interview you separately."

"Detective Delafield, I understand your reasons for that." The older woman's eyes were fastened on Aimee. "But is it absolutely necessary?"

Kate looked at Aimee Grant. Clearly, she was in shock, and Paula Grant did not want to be separated from her. But just as clearly, her own duty lay with the dead man in the other room, and separate interviews were recommended procedure in order to glean each person's individual memory. Taylor, who had preceded her here and had talked to the patrol officers, shrugged almost imperceptibly. Kate nodded at Paula Grant; she would initiate the interview, and see what developed.

She took a few moments to glance around the apartment. A boomerang-shaped glass coffee table seemed to rest lightly on chrome supports, its surface pristine save for a large brass ashtray with a cigarette case beside it, a drink on a coaster, and a tall, slender, highly stylized pewter sculpture of a female nude. Two large marble-topped end tables and a plant table were stacked with books and magazines. Three sling chairs made of good leather faced a gray tweed sofa. Another sling chair, this one of wood and canvas, appeared to be an authentic director's chair: the name DOROTHY ARZNER was stencilled across its back. This chair was not to be sat upon; it reposed in a place of honor below a black-framed poster of Joan Crawford in a film Kate had never heard of, *The Bride Wore Red*.

More than a dozen similarly framed posters and movie photo montages adorned the walls. Kate's glance sped in surprised recognition: Shirley McLaine and Audrey Hepburn in *The Children's Hour*. Candice Bergen as Lakey in *The Group*. Susan Sarandon and

Catherine Deneuve in *The Hunger.* Garbo, in sculptured black and white androgyny, in *Queen Christina.* Mariel Hemingway and Patrice Donnelly soaring over a track hurdle in *Personal Best.* A bar scene with the two female stars of *Lianna.* And on the dining room wall, Helen Shaver looking bemusedly into the distance as Patricia Charbonneau leaned back confidently against a Chevy convertible in *Desert Hearts.*

Kate glanced at Taylor to see if he had discerned the connection between most of these posters. He was fixated on the poster of Joan Crawford.

He asked Paula Grant, "You have something to do with all these movies?"

"A few," she said in her husky voice. "The one you're looking at, Dorothy Arzner directed in 'thirty-seven. My mother was in the costume department at MGM and was privileged to be assigned to her picture — I was fourteen at the time."

Paula Grant's explanation did not quite account for her evident adulation of Arzner. But Kate could guess: fourteen was the age when she herself had had her first serious sexual attraction, to a woman teacher . . .

Paula Grant gestured to the other posters with a finely boned, translucent hand. "Most of these are after my time in the industry. I simply like them for . . . various reasons."

She brought her gaze back to fix it acutely on Kate, and Kate understood that Paula Grant had missed nothing of her own survey of the posters.

Kate sat in one of the leather sling chairs, Taylor beside her. Paula and Aimee Grant settled themselves on the sofa. Smoothing her windbreaker as best she could, Kate pulled out her notebook and commanded herself to focus on her notes and the detail she needed to gain from this interview.

"I realize this is very difficult," she began. She inhaled a faint scent of lavender, whether from one of the Grants, or the apartment itself, she was unsure. "But my partner and I need to have you take us through the events of today."

She looked up. Aimee Grant's blue-violet eyes were on her in unfocused vulnerability.

Taylor said, "Maybe we could start with when you discovered the victim." Kate heard the impatience in his voice and understood it. They had too much to do, and too quickly, to afford all this wasted motion.

"At five minutes to six," Paula Grant answered with regal calm. "Aimee had arrived earlier today, and we were leaving for dinner."

Aimee Grant said softly, "Aunt Paula was determined to go in there and see what was wrong."

"So *why* did you go in there?" Taylor prompted. "You hear sounds from his apartment?"

"Quite the contrary," said Paula Grant. "And this is what I'm afraid will be very hard to explain — it was because of the sounds I *didn't* hear." She shook her head as if wearied by the thought of trying to be understood.

"Ms. Grant," Kate said, "Detective Taylor and I will be in charge of this investigation —"

"Will you indeed," Paula Grant said, glancing at Kate with sharp interest.

"— And we need you to go over everything very carefully, in as much detail as you can remember."

"Since my niece and I are both Ms. Grant," Paula

Grant noted, "it seems easier to call us Paula and Aimee." She added, "I went into Owen Sinclair's apartment because his door was open — but mostly because there was a change in the *walla.*"

Kate and Taylor exchanged perplexed glances. Aimee Grant's face slowly eased into a faint smile.

Paula leaned to the coffee table and withdrew a long, slender cigarette from her black leather cigarette case. "And to explain what *walla* means, I have to further explain that I was a script supervisor before I left the industry." She looked at Taylor. "Do you know what a script supervisor does?"

Taylor crossed an ankle over a knee and propped his notebook in his lap. "Things like making sure some actor isn't wearing a blue shirt in a scene when he's supposed to have on a white one," he said comfortably.

"Yes. But that's equivalent to my defining police work as giving traffic tickets," Paula said with equal ease. "A script supervisor has to monitor everything — dialogue, makeup, hairstyles, props, set dressings — not to mention sequence and camera angles for the benefit of the film editor."

"A mountain of detail," Kate commented, impressed.

"Truly. A script supervisor on a movie set has to carry so many tools of her trade she looks like a Sherpa guide." Paula lit her cigarette with a slender gold lighter. Tucking the lighter back into the cigarette case, she said, "Unless a scene is photographed without sound she also has to match what we call *presence,* or *roomtone* — like the sounds in a restaurant. And then there's unscripted, constant background that's recorded to give a particular scene realism. Like street noise, or birds or night insects. That's called *walla*."

The smoke from Paula's cigarette swirled as she gestured toward Owen Sinclair's apartment. "Music came out of there his every waking moment. I have an extra bedroom between this room and his apartment, but I still hear it — heard it — constantly. It was the *walla* of my daily life."

"It was really loud today," Aimee interjected. "The man was a big, loud, inconsiderate jerk. A *creep.*"

"Just before Aimee and I were leaving for dinner," Paula continued unperturbed, "his music stopped. And there was no reason for it to stop."

Taylor shook his head. "I don't get it."

Nor did Kate. She asked, "Couldn't he have simply left the apartment? Didn't he turn off his music when he went out?"

"Of course. But I always heard his door slam, even if I was in the shower. He never left his apartment without slamming the door off the hinges."

"Never?" Taylor asked skeptically.

"Never."

"Paula," Kate said, "please tell us exactly what happened as you went out to dinner." She had further questions about Paula Grant's *walla*, but Taylor had become prematurely argumentative.

"Some instinct — I don't know what it was, except I felt something was wrong — something drew me down the hall to his apartment. I sensed . . . Well, the door was open and Aimee and I looked in —"

"The door," Kate interrupted, writing rapidly, "how far was it open?"

"About this much," Aimee said, bracing her hands about two feet apart.

"Yes," Paula said. "Then I called out to him."

"What did you say?"

Paula looked at her in annoyance. "What anyone would say. 'Owen, are you there?' Then I went in."

"I didn't want her to," Aimee said.

"I had to," Paula said. "I *knew* something was wrong." She began to flick at a speck of something on her immaculate beige trousers.

"If you thought something was wrong," Taylor said, "didn't you think a criminal might still be in there?"

"I thought so," Aimee said. "I said so."

Paula's cigarette smoke made more curls as she gestured dismissal of this suggestion. "His door wasn't damaged, and that's the only way anyone can break into an apartment on this floor. We've never had an instance of crime in the twenty-five years I've lived here. I simply thought he was in trouble."

"What kind of trouble?" Taylor asked.

She said with ill-concealed impatience, "Illness, of course. He hasn't been all that well lately. So I went in."

"And I followed," Aimee said. She was sitting perfectly still; her eyes again looked unfocused.

"I went down the hallway to his bedroom . . ." The low voice had fallen a tone deeper.

"I know this is very difficult," Kate offered.

"When I saw what was in the bedroom I tried to shield Aimee . . ."

"Those eyes," Aimee whispered. "He was dead, I had to get out of there —"

Kate watched the older woman reach to the

23

younger one and pat her hand. Paula's hand was the same long slender shape as Aimee's, but the age difference between the two women was suddenly conspicuous in the greater complexity of emotion on the older woman's face, a handsome face matured like a cliffside after years of summer suns and winter rains.

"I guess I screamed," Aimee said. "The landlady and some other tenants came running down the hall, and I wanted someone to go in after Aunt Paula but then she came out —"

Kate asked, "Do you know if anybody else went in the apartment afterward, before police officers arrived?"

"No," Paula answered. "I wouldn't allow it. Not out of any sense of duty to the police. I couldn't have anyone see what we saw. I closed the door and made everyone go down to the first floor until the officers arrived."

Kate asked quietly of both women, "At that point you believed the victim was dead?"

Aimee looked stricken. "I never —"

Again Paula patted Aimee's hand. "He indeed was dead. I checked. I —" She put her cigarette on the ashtray and picked up the drink from the coffee table and sipped from it. "I went to him, felt for a pulse in the neck." Her slender shoulders were rigidly straight; the hand holding the drink was slightly tremulous.

Remembering the bloody-eyed apparition in the bedroom next door, Kate looked at Paula Grant with deepening respect. The strength in this woman was as much a matter of will as a natural attribute.

Paula said evenly, "I saw how he was handcuffed. I turned to pick up the phone to call the police right then, but I saw the cord was cut. I didn't touch anything, do anything more — I simply left. By then I was very frightened."

"Anyone would be," Kate murmured. She asked, "What you saw — did you mention any details to the other tenants?"

"Only that he was dead, that someone had done something terrible to him. Nothing more."

"Paula," Taylor said, "while you were in the apartment, did you happen to look in any of the other rooms?"

"No," she answered. Her eyes widened; there was an almost imperceptible shudder in the thin body. "Do you mean you think someone . . . could have . . ."

"Not likely," Kate told her. "You found the door open. A criminal wouldn't ordinarily draw attention to himself by leaving a door open while he was inside." She asked, "Had you previously been in Mr. Sinclair's apartment?"

"On rare occasions. He had a Fourth of July open house — I felt obliged to make an appearance. I believe that was the last time."

As Kate made a note of this hint of animosity, she casually led Paula Grant with an open-ended question: "What can you tell us about Mr. Sinclair?"

"What do you need to know?"

Kate smothered a smile. So much for Paula Grant's willingness to volunteer information. "How long have you known him?"

Paula sipped her drink, reflecting. Aimee, evidently

25

deciding that her contribution to this interview was concluded, rose and moved around the room, hands stuffed in the pockets of her black pants.

Paula said, "I've lived here since early 'sixty-three. Owen moved in after me — I'm not sure, perhaps a year or two later. After this length of time it's difficult to remember exactly."

Taylor asked, "You lived next to him all this time?"

"I had an apartment on the first floor briefly. Then Alice Goldstein and I shared this larger apartment for the next nineteen years. Until Alice's death five years ago." She had addressed her answer to Kate, in flat expressionless tones that proscribed further inquiry.

Thinking that Taylor had surely noticed Paula Grant's closed face, her distant tone, and her shunning of such euphemisms as friend or roommate with respect to Alice Goldstein, Kate edged the interview away from this topic. "You talked about the *walla* created by Mr. Sinclair's music. Did it not bother you enough to complain?"

Paula stiffened, clearly provoked by the question. "Of course it bothered me enough to complain. Do you think I spend my days comatose? Complaining was useless — either to him or Hazel. Hazel Turner," she clarified icily, "the landlady."

Taylor asked incredulously, "You're saying you put up with the victim's loud music for twenty-four *years?*"

"Of course not. Only since the advent of rent control. That's when Owen realized he could safely abandon any sort of consideration for anyone."

Paula's voice was caustic. "Myself, Maxine across the hall, Mildred in the apartment below — he knew moving from here would cause any one of us great financial hardship. And as for Hazel — she knows she can charge much higher rents for our apartments if we move."

Another bully, Kate thought. Sinclair was just another bully abusing whatever petty power he managed to get his hands on. She asked, "Did you ever think of calling the police?"

"Mildred did. Once. They as much as said we were a collection of old crocks."

Kate was too occupied with her fury to speak. Taylor said, "You say you left for dinner at five minutes to six —"

"Not precisely for dinner. We were going over first to pay a visit to some relatives."

Calm again, Kate asked, "Whenever you leave this apartment, which staircase do you ordinarily use, the front or the rear?"

"The front, of course. I use the back stairs only to go down to the laundry room."

"When you went into Mr. Sinclair's apartment, did you perhaps smell anything?"

She reflected. "Nothing out of the ordinary."

Aimee interjected, "Only his putrid cigar smoke."

"Paula," Kate said, "do you know anything about Mr. Sinclair that may help us find who is responsible for his death?"

"I assume you mean any enemies of his." She shrugged. "He'd acquired plenty of those — just from the kind of man he was." She shrugged again. "I've fervently wished him dead myself. But I don't know

27

anyone who would do something like . . . that. I think all of us at times wish certain people dead. But we don't do anything about it."

"Some of us do," Taylor said, writing in his notebook.

"I've never been able to imagine anyone who can," Paula told him. "But obviously someone he knew well did that to him."

"Why do you think so?" Taylor asked the question almost idly, but Kate knew better, knew he was following his own scents in this interview.

"Someone had to fasten that handcuff to him. Someone cut the phone cord. But no one broke in. So Owen had to open his door to someone he knew."

Taylor did not respond, nor did Kate. There were methods of entering that did not involve breaking in, but all such possibilities had to remain between herself and Taylor at this early stage of the investigation. Kate asked, "Did you hear anyone knock on his door?"

"No, but he has a doorbell. And my television was on, Aimee was watching a very noisy football game for part of the afternoon."

Taylor asked, "When did you last see Mr. Sinclair alive?"

"The same as everyone else — at the party."

"Party?" Kate inquired, remembering evidence of a gathering in the community room on the first floor.

"Hazel's Thanksgiving get-together. Most of us who were home dropped in for some time at least. Owen did, too."

"How long did you stay?" Taylor inquired.

"I'm not sure. I talked for a time to Dorothy

Brennan — she's lived here less than a year." Paula looked over at Aimee. "How long do you think we were downstairs, dear?"

Aimee was leaning against the wall adjacent to them, her arms crossed. "I watched most of the first half of the Dallas game on the TV down there. I'd say maybe an hour and a half."

Kate asked, "Was Mr. Sinclair there as well during that time?"

"I don't remember," Aimee said. "I tried to ignore him."

Paula closed her eyes to concentrate. "He came in after we arrived. He left before we did. I do remember now — he wasn't feeling well again."

Kate exchanged glances with Taylor. There were even more compelling reasons now to collect the debris from that party downstairs. She turned to a fresh page in her notebook. "Could you tell us who was at the party?"

Paula said with a trace of tartness, "I was a script supervisor, remember? Memory like an elephant." She gave Kate and Taylor eight names in addition to herself and Aimee.

Paula Grant's face suddenly looked gaunt with tiredness, and Kate decided to conclude the interview. She said, "We appreciate your cooperation."

Paula said wearily, "This is only the beginning, isn't it."

"I'm sorry," Kate said softly. "But yes, I'm sure we'll have other questions as the investigation develops. We'll need to prepare a statement for you to sign."

Paula nodded, and Kate said, "It's very important

that you keep to yourselves every detail of what you saw in Mr. Sinclair's apartment, everything you've discussed with us. That will really help."

Again Paula Grant nodded. She rose as the two detectives got to their feet. Aimee Grant, leaning against the wall near the poster of *The Children's Hour*, was staring intently at Kate.

– 3 –

Two attendants in brown jumpsuits, CORONER stitched in yellow letters across their backs, waited placidly beside a stretcher outside Owen Sinclair's apartment. Kate and Taylor again entered the living room of the apartment, Kate glimpsing strobe flashes in the dining alcove, visual echoes from where Shapiro photographed the kitchen. Baker, she assumed, was still fingerprinting the bedroom at the end of the hall.

She inquired of Taylor, "Any ideas so far?"

"Gonna be a walk through," he said.

Surprised by this confident assertion, she turned to him. "How so?"

"Paula just gave it to us." His broad face hardening, Taylor surveyed the stereo and tape equipment crowding the room. "His goddam music making that goddam racket day and night —" He jabbed a hand toward the murder scene in the back bedroom. "The son of a bitch ever did that to me I'd decorate this whole damn apartment with his face. He figured three old ladies couldn't do one damn thing to him. But one of 'em figured out how to air-mail his ass."

Kate nodded, not in agreement with Taylor's hypothesis but in support of his angry contempt for the bully Owen Sinclair had been in life. She said, "I'd like to know which of our people answered Mildred's five-eighty-six."

Taylor shrugged. "Loud noise complaints are a royal pain, Kate. I used to hate those calls. Mostly people so tanked up they'd just as soon shoot you as not. I see how our people figured these old ladies for cranks. But I gotta say Paula's blowing smoke about not killing somebody over loud music." Taylor tapped the spine of his notebook against a tall dust-coated speaker in loud, arrhythmic demonstration as he continued, "You can like dogs, but let one bark long enough and by God you'll poison it to shut it up."

Kate nodded somberly, remembering child abuse cases she had seen in Juvenile — the perpetrators — mothers under stress, whose emotional control had snapped over the incessant crying of their babies. But premeditated murder was something else, and sitting down to watch the grisly, ghastly manner in which Owen Sinclair had died was something else again.

"Ed," she said, "the handcuffs, the chair beside the bed —"

"Yeah. I know, Kate. I figure he let one of those women in before he got real sick, and when he had his bad convulsions he'd be easy enough for anybody to cuff and leave to croak. I figure we're as likely wrong as right about why the chair was there."

"Maybe." But every instinct in her proclaimed the grim purpose of that chair beside that bed. Let Taylor nurse his improbable theory, she would not argue with him — not for some time yet. She knew too well how he would withdraw his attention from a case for which he had lost his eagerness, to go through only the bureaucratic motions required of him. Allowing him to follow his own scents would keep his nose on the trail.

"Paula said Sinclair started all this business when rent control came in," she mused. "That was when, around nineteen-eighty or so —" She broke off, appalled. "Ed, that's eight *years* ago."

Taylor was pushing his fleshy lips in and out. "Eight years of the Chinese water torture, Kate. We're gonna end up collaring one of these three old ladies I guarantee you." In a tone that held something like concession he offered, "But Paula, that's one classy lady."

Too classy to be a vicious killer, she was about to suggest, but took back the words. Women seldom killed, but they did indeed kill. And the unlikeliest people could be the most rabid killers.

"And that niece of hers," Taylor continued. "That one's a real barn burner."

Kate looked at him.

"A ten." As Kate sifted in puzzlement through her images of Aimee Grant, Taylor stared at her in open surprise. "For chrissakes," he said in exasperation, "*good-looking.*"

"I see," she said. But she had not seen. Her perceptions of Paula Grant had been so dominant that she had not absorbed more than a nebulous physical impression of the younger woman.

Taylor, his blond eyebrows raised, was shaking his head, and she looked at him in smothered amusement. How could she, of all people, fail to notice what he deemed an unusually beautiful woman? Of course it was all part of his unspoken awareness that she was a lesbian. And if he could not deal with his discomfort over her sexual nature, he could not possibly understand that of the two women, Paula Grant was the one she found unusually beautiful.

Turning away from him, she took time to review the last details she had recorded of the death scene surroundings. Drapes drawn and no windows open; no appliances in use save the refrigerator; lights on only in the living room and at the death scene itself. Ashtrays had been emptied but not wiped clean. The kitchen showed no evidence of a meal having been eaten nor one in any phase of preparation. Sinclair had been handcuffed to his bed, but there was no sign anywhere of a struggle.

Shapiro now crouched in the dining room, his camera flashing, and Kate moved past him into the small kitchen. She had already noted a small formica table, its red plastic chair a match of the one in the bedroom. She now examined an assortment of liquor

34

bottles on the counter next to the refrigerator. An unopened and dusty fifth of Cutty Sark Scotch, two quarts of Jim Beam, one of them 100 proof and three-quarters empty, an unopened Harper's, a half-empty half gallon of Ten High. So Sinclair had been a bourbon drinker, the Ten High apparently his customary brand. And judging by the efficient and unabashed proximity of his liquor to glasses and ice cubes, and the assortment of glasses at the death scene, he had been a steady if not hard drinker. But a drinker seemingly with sense enough not to smoke in bed: there were neither smoking materials nor an ashtray in his bedroom.

As Taylor joined her, Kate wedged open the cabinet below the chipped and brown-stained sink with her pen. Along with cleaning materials and sponges was a plastic-lined trash can, empty. Apparently Sinclair — or someone — had very recently taken out the garbage. She said to Taylor, "Let's check with Hansen, be sure he's taped off the building's trash."

She opened other cabinets with the pen, and glanced over glasses and coffee mugs, a set of orangish Melmac dishes so old the flower pattern was scratched and faded. A few battered pots and pans, and canned food, mostly soup, spaghetti, beans, and Dinty Moore stew, and cereal and Ritz crackers and Folger's instant coffee. And three more half gallons of Ten High.

Taylor used his own pen to pry open a yellowing Coldspot refrigerator. A half-full plastic gallon of water, a loaf of rye bread and three packages of lunch meat, bottles of ketchup, mustard, mayonnaise and pickles, four cans of Budweiser. The freezer

35

section held four Swanson TV dinners and a plastic sack of ice cubes.

She was depressed by this room, so typical of a person living alone and indifferent to diet. The kitchen in her own apartment was shiny and modern and much better equipped, but the bleak neatness of this room was too much like it in spirit.

"Get outta here," growled Baker, placing his large case of fingerprinting apparatus on the kitchen floor.

"We didn't touch a thing," Taylor answered.

"Get outta here," he repeated, turning his narrow, black-shirted back to them.

Taylor went off to consult with Hansen about the building's trash, and Kate walked into the back bedroom where Everson was closing up his medical bag.

The arched, bloody-eyed corpse on the bed was outlined in tape in preparation for its removal. The handcuffs which had fastened Owen Sinclair to his death bed lay beside him in a plastic evidence bag, and Kate picked up the bag by its top, to heft it. The cuffs were lighter than her own, and black. Very possibly they could be traced by lot number through their manufacturer . . .

She glanced over the room. Gray fingerprint powder covered every surface. The red plastic chair and the phone were gone, presumably packed and loaded in Baker's van for transport to the lab. Elimination points from the tenants would be necessary . . .

Everson, arms crossed, was watching her. She gestured to the bed. "All yours."

"Fresh meat for our friendly sausage shop," he

said cheerily. "The autopsy figures to be Saturday." And he left the room to summon the attendants with the stretcher.

Notification of next of kin was now a priority, and Kate asked Baker to dust the ancient leather address book in the living room so that she could examine it. But Sinclair's entries on the dog-eared pages were cryptic — mostly first names and sometimes simply initials with a phone number and only occasionally an address. The "S" section where she had expected to see Sinclair relatives listed had been ripped out, and some time ago, judging by the yellowed jagged remains of the page. She bagged the address book in plastic and marked it as evidence.

In the bedroom with its empty mattress taped in the stark curve of Owen Sinclair's corpse, she assigned Taylor to examine Sinclair's clothing. She made a preliminary inspection of three cardboard file boxes behind the sliding door of the room's wall-to-wall closet.

The boxes were stuffed with artifacts of Sinclair's life. Hundreds of photographs, letters and postcards; scrapbooks of yellowed newspaper and magazine clippings all apparently related to movies Sinclair had been involved with; three bound copies of plays, their author Owen Charles Sinclair; escrow papers on property sold decades ago; a crumpled manila envelope holding four sets of divorce papers from four different women.

"Nothing here," Taylor told her, searching through polo shirts and shorts in the lower drawer of Sinclair's dresser.

"It'll take hours to sift through what we've got in these boxes," Kate told him. "He's been divorced so many times it's hard to say who's next of kin."

"I say we find out what the landlady knows," Taylor said.

Hazel Turner's tight, pink-toned bleached curls seemed corkscrewed into her head. Her blue eyes darted over Kate, then fastened on her ID. "A woman detective," she rumbled, as if Taylor's body occupied no visible space. One liver-spotted hand holding a cigarette, the other deep in the huge patch pocket of her navy blue housecoat, she stepped back from her doorway. "Well, come in, dear. You too," she added, conceding Taylor's existence.

Her steel-framed glasses partway down her long thin nose, she was still scrutinizing Kate. "You're a good size for a woman in the police, you look very capable."

"Size isn't really a necessity in police work," Kate answered courteously, reflecting that she had made a better impression on Hazel Turner than she had on Paula Grant.

Glancing over the living room she wondered if it had been furnished with the confiscated belongings of evicted tenants. It was gorged with furniture: a mismatched sofa and loveseat combined with four dissimilar chairs, five tables holding an assortment of lamps casting low wattage pools of orange light, three overflowing magazine racks, a bedraggled corn plant, two television sets, each tuned to a different station, the sound off. The walls were a pastiche of murky landscapes and English hunting scenes. Against the far window, two waist-high ceramic labrador retrievers flanked a dimly visible roll-top desk buried under a blizzard of paper, presumably records of the affairs of the Beverly Malibu. The apartment smelled of decades of cigarette smoke and cooking, a complexity of odors ingrained into the walls like coal dust into pores.

Kate asked, "May we sit down, Ms. Turner?"

"Hazel. I'm Hazel, dear." She sank into the gold corduroy sofa. "I'd rather have a fine big policewoman like you in my corner than some little bitty thing. Or," she added, tapping her cigarette on a tiny china ashtray, "some clumsy male."

Taylor chose a whitish-gray overstuffed armchair, then jerked back as a white Persian cat leaped from its depths onto the carpet. The cat turned, raised its ruffled and indignant tail to Taylor, and stalked disdainfully from the room.

"You mustn't mind Precious," Hazel said. "She's really very sweet."

Taylor turned to another chair, this one of lacquered wood with an upholstered seat, and gingerly settled his bulk into it. Kate, as she sat on the apple-green loveseat, looked at him in sympathy; so far he was receiving exceedingly short shrift from most of the females in this apartment.

"Ever since Jerome passed on, Precious has just taken over the place. Why, she even —"

"Ma'am," Taylor said softly, "we need to —"

"You don't have to tell me," Hazel said in her gravelly voice. She put down her cigarette and reached to the coffee table to a tiny, stoppered,

39

luminous green vase covered with silver filigree. She clutched it, then released it. "Such a dreadful shock . . ."

Kate said, "Mr. Sinclair lived here a number of years, we understand. Did you know him well enough to tell us who his next of kin might be?"

"Well now, that's a good question, isn't it?" She shook her pink-toned head. "He's got ex-wives a-plenty and three daughters, one of 'em up north, they haven't shown up here in maybe ten years or more. His youngest boy was the apple of his eye, he got back from over there in Vietnam, he died of bowel cancer not even one year later. Twenty-four years of age, now isn't that just something?"

So this was the young man in the photo in Owen Sinclair's apartment. Kate said, "If you could help us out, we need to notify —"

"Well, I made a few phone calls myself right after the police came," Hazel admitted. "Vivian, that's the second wife, the one that had his kids, she lives in Hollywood. And there's some friends that knew Owen and my Jerome from the old days. The way news travels in this town, everybody knows all about this by now." She gestured to the flickering, silent TV sets. "Better they shouldn't find out from there. They'd know the building, lots of people in this town know all about the Beverly Malibu."

Taylor looked at Kate, his expression questioning. Was Hazel Turner lunatic enough to actually believe that this ordinary building was somehow distinguishable from thousands of similar structures in Los Angeles? Kate remembered Hansen's remark: *She's got a very big mouth.* This woman could be a trove of information.

Kate nodded encouragement at Hazel. "How did Vivian take the news?" she asked, interested in the ex-wife who did not sufficiently care about Owen Sinclair's death to come over to the famous Beverly Malibu apartment building.

"I was plain shocked." Adjusting her glasses, Hazel assembled her features into an expression appropriate to her words, and picked up her cigarette. "I mean, you've got to have *some* respect for the dead. But she said the world was a better place without him. She don't mean anything by it. She'd had a few, I could tell."

"Could you give us Vivian's address and phone number?" Taylor asked, picking several long white hairs from his trousers.

"You can get it the same place I always do. Right in the phone book, under Vivian Sinclair. On Mariposa in Hollywood. But she hasn't had one thing to do with him for years, if that's what you're driving at. For sure she wasn't here today."

Hazel's voice sounded like pebbles washed by water: "Is it true what Paula told us? I own this building, I have a right to know. She said something was done to Owen. Is that so?"

At Kate's glance and brief head-shake, Taylor maintained his silence.

She studied Hazel Turner. The woman could not be much older than Paula Grant. How very differently people aged . . . Paula seemed younger and so much more vital . . . Still, Hazel Turner was equal to Paula Grant as a source of information, and her willing cooperation was essential.

"We'll tell you what we can, Hazel." What she would say now would be in the papers tomorrow anyway, if not on the late news tonight. She looked directly into the landlady's eyes. "It does appear he was a victim of homicide." The sharpness faded from the blue eyes looking into Kate's, as if in flight from the words. "It appears he was poisoned."

Hazel's hand flew to her throat as if she were experiencing the symptoms in herself. Then she seized the stoppered green vase on the coffee table. "Jerome, are you listening to this?" Holding the container at arm's length, glaring at it, she shook it fiercely. "Are you hearing what's happened in this sorry building you got us into? See what's happened now because you bought a half block from Beverly Hills? In Beverly Hills this never happens and your poor widow can get decent rents and be living with the best kind of people and there'd be decent streets and decent police —" She broke off and looked at Kate. "Not meaning you dear, of course."

Taylor was staring at Hazel, a corner of his mouth beginning to uncontrollably twitch. With effort Kate looked back at Hazel and the filigreed urn, trying to keep her own face expressionless.

She studied the urn, puzzled. It looked too small, in her experience, to be the receptacle of anything more than a child's ashes. She cleared her throat and returned to the subject of Owen Sinclair's ex-wife. "You say you're sure Vivian Sinclair wasn't here today. How can you be so sure?"

"I saw everybody that came and went." Hazel put the urn on the coffee table and stubbed out her cigarette. She seemed suddenly shrunken, her shapeless body drooping in the navy blue housecoat as if deflated from the impact of Kate's disclosure.

"From early this morning I was back and forth all the time from here to the community room cleaning up, getting everything ready." The voice sounded even more watery. "I tell you, I saw everybody that came and went."

Taylor suggested, "Maybe somebody came in without you hearing them, maybe when you were back there?" He gestured to the dark nether regions of the apartment.

Hazel's body snapped erect. "Even if I don't see somebody, I hear them. I've been in this apartment thirty-five years, Mister Detective, I know what goes on in my building. There's this piece of tile just inside the lobby door that clanks, there's a board in the stairway that squeaks when you go upstairs. I hear everybody whether I want to or not."

And you want to, Kate thought. And lucky for us that you do. She turned to a fresh page in her notebook. "We believe you, Hazel. Would you tell us exactly who you did see, and when?"

"Well, I can tell you the who. But the when's not so easy. I *was* busy, you see. Lorraine left early. That's Lorraine Rothberg. So did Cliffie Stone. And Diane what's her name, she's new here, Diane Sweeney. And then Sue McFee. Then Theo DeRosa's two sons came to collect him in their butterfly net. And then that lovely girl came in, Paula's niece. And then —" Her tiny, pink-lipsticked mouth pursed in disapproval. "Then that smart-alecky black friend of Cyril's."

Kate was writing rapidly. "Your party started when, Hazel?"

"Noon. Sue and Lorraine stopped in for a few

minutes then went off about their business. Then everybody else began showing up, maybe one o'clock or so."

"What time did Mr. Sinclair appear?"

She knitted her brow, then shook her head. "Don't remember. I was busy, you see, taking care of everything."

Kate shifted her position on the loveseat and mentally braced herself. "What did you serve at your party?"

"A nice wedge of cheddar and some lovely corned beef and pastrami right from Nate 'n Al's, potato salad, fresh vegetables and my special dip, my special recipe for wine punch —"

Hazel's eyes widened and her hand again flew to her throat as the full import of Kate's question struck her. "Poison! Why, you don't —"

She launched herself from the sofa and marched through the living room and into the dark interior of the apartment.

"Jesus Christ," Taylor uttered, "now what's she doing? Getting a gun?" He shifted, to better reach the holster at his hip.

"More likely she'll force us to eat the leftover food to prove it's not poisoned," Kate suggested with a grin. "Listen, Ed, we need to get on the phone to Vivian Sinclair and verify about next-of-kin before it gets much later —"

Hazel reappeared carrying three urns identical to the one sitting on the coffee table. She set them down with an emphatic *whack* and formed all four into a tight square. "Now, Jerome, you just listen to what they're saying and what you got us into with this godforsaken building."

44

"Hazel —" Kate did not dare look at Taylor. She cleared her throat. "Those urns all contain the ashes of your husband?"

"Every worthless flake," she said grimly.

Taylor was gaping at the green urns. "Four of them?"

"One for in here, one for the bedroom, one for the dining room, one for the bathroom. I got tired of carrying him room to room. So I got these and put him in every room. I get him all together when we need a council of war."

Taylor leaned toward her in his most tolerant and reassuring manner. "Hazel, all we're trying to do right now is piece together what happened and how."

She glared at him. "You think there was something in my food!"

"If that were the case," Kate added her own reassurance, "then it seems others besides Mr. Sinclair would be affected. But we have to evaluate all possibilities. And I caution you, Hazel — don't eat or drink *anything* left over from the party. We may need to take some of it for testing."

"I *know* it wasn't my food. And I *know* who was here today and who wasn't — and one of us did this terrible thing to Owen." She shook a finger at the assembly of green urns. "Somebody in this godforsaken building you foisted on me, Jerome!" The finger shook at Kate. "Somebody in our Beverly Malibu did this and you better find out who it is plenty quick. I run a decent —"

"Tell us," Kate interrupted, "did Mr. Sinclair eat any of the food?"

"Like he hadn't eaten in a month." Peering resentfully over her glasses at Kate, she sat back in the sofa and lit another cigarette. "Never was a thing wrong with Owen's appetite — for anything. He even brought down his own bourbon, said my wine punch didn't have enough oomph to it." She added tartly, "But it had oomph enough that he asked me to bring some up to his place for his awful July the Fourth shindig."

Without looking at Taylor Kate knew he was thinking the same thing as she: they would collect those open liquor bottles in Owen Sinclair's apartment. She asked, "When did Mr. Sinclair leave the party today?"

Hazel frowned. "Don't know. Can't remember."

"Do you remember who he spent any time with during the party?"

"Well . . . Dudley Kincaid. The two of them got to arguing as usual with Parker. Parker Thomas. And Cyril Crane. And it seems to me Dorothy Brennan was in there too, but more likely she was just listening, she's such a friendly one."

"Not —" Kate consulted her notes. "Not Mildred or Paula or Maxine?"

Scrutinizing Kate, Hazel shook her head.

Approaching this uncharacteristic reticence carefully, Kate said, "We understand there was a bit of bad feeling between Mr. Sinclair and those three women."

Hazel sighed. "I guess you know about it then. Bad feeling don't hardly say it. Owen had a side to him that bothered a few folks here. They tried to get me into all their squabbles but I wouldn't do it. Owen, he's lived here for years . . . and we're all

46

grownups, after all." She addressed the urns: "Jerome, didn't you always say grownups should be able to settle their own differences?" She returned her attention to Kate. "Anybody that don't like the Beverly Malibu, they can move out. That's their privilege. And I can maybe get a friendlier tenant and the rent due me besides. Ever since this abomination they call rent control —" The blue eyes had ignited. "I run a decent building, I deserve decent —"

It was Taylor's turn to interrupt. "Who besides Maxine and Mildred and Paula had run-ins with him?"

Hazel let go of her outrage with obvious reluctance. "Well . . . Cyril. And Lorraine, but she wasn't here today. And Parker Thomas, he's never had any use for him at all."

Kate asked, "Do you have parties for your tenants very often?"

Hazel put her cigarette on the ashtray, waving away a plume of smoke that drifted toward the green urns. "On the holidays. Lots of people here are pretty much alone. In a manner of speaking I still have Jerome with me —" She passed her hand over the urns like a benediction. "But it still gets awfully hard around the holidays."

What was hardest for herself about the holidays, Kate thought, was dealing with the generous impulses of those who believed that she was deprived, and that the shared glow of their own attachments would patch over her deprivation. Even Taylor had not been immune. From the way he was looking away from her now, he felt guilty that he had not offered to share his family with her on this Thanksgiving Day. She knew she would have to deal with an insistent invitation from him for Christmas.

She said to Hazel, "Why do you have parties for tenants you want to get rid of?"

"I never said I wanted to get rid of them," Hazel retorted. "There's some tenants lived here as long as I have. The Beverly Malibu's their home just as much as mine. I wouldn't raise their rents sky high or do one thing to them. But a person shouldn't be *ordered* what to charge for their own private property. You own a building, you shouldn't ought to be *told* how to run things."

Kate thought: But so many landlords wouldn't share your sentiment for their tenants. She asked, "Have you ever expressed any of these thoughts to your older tenants?"

"I'm not crazy," Hazel snapped. "And you better not repeat one word of what I'm telling you here, I'm only telling because you're the police." She aimed her glare of warning at Kate, then Taylor, and back. "The tenants, they'd all just take advantage. They'd nag me to death for new carpets, they'd want paint and new stoves, God knows what all."

"You mentioned Mr. Sinclair's Fourth of July party," Kate said, trying to smother her amused liking for Hazel Turner. "From that I take it he did mix somewhat with the other tenants?"

"Some. But that Fourth of July thing wasn't what you'd call a party at all, not like mine today. I told him to use the community room but oh no, it was too much trouble, he just wanted folks in for a few drinks in that gloomy place of his. What a mess. All he had was my wine punch to go with his measly potato chips and pretzels and his stinking bourbon. The other tenants were in and out of that place in no time. Paula couldn't turn her nose up high enough." She sniffed. "She's too snooty by half, that one."

"Who all was there?" Kate asked.

She shrugged. "Can't really remember. Most anybody that was here, I suppose. If they were home they dropped in for a time."

Kate thought: Paula Grant with her script supervisor memory will know more details of that party. "Hazel," she said, "let's go back to the time before and after the party today. You say you know everybody who came into the building, correct?"

Hazel nodded. "Any tenant that ever buzzes somebody in without knowing who it is gets a royal piece of my mind, I don't mind telling you. In these times it could be some gang that'll spray graffiti or even bullets all over your walls, or some bible-thumper trying to —"

Kate interrupted, "Could anyone get into the building other than through the front door? There are gates alongside the building."

"Padlocked," the landlady said grimly.

"Somebody could climb over," Taylor pointed out.

"They still couldn't get in. I'm just as careful about that back door as the front one. When Owen lost his keys I had that lock changed right along with the front door even though he yelled his head off about it."

Kate looked at her with acute interest. "When did all this happen?"

"That very same July the Fourth party. He swore his keys must of got swept up and tossed out with the party trash, but I couldn't take a chance believing him, I had to get the front and back door locks changed the very next day and I had him pay the bill for that and everybody's new keys, it was his fault after all."

Kate asked, "Since the key to Mr. Sinclair's apartment was also lost, I assume you changed that lock as well?"

She shook her head. "He was mad as the devil, claimed it didn't matter at all." She shrugged. "If he wanted to take a chance on somebody stealing his things, it was up to him."

Kate took some time over her notes, and looked up to find Hazel Turner slumped down in the sofa and completing a yawn. Kate glanced at her watch: eleven-thirty. Catching Taylor's eye she pantomimed holding a phone to her ear.

He got up with alacrity to make the necessary phone call to Vivian Sinclair. "Excuse me, Hazel," he said, brushing more white hairs from his trousers. "Kate, I'll see you upstairs."

Ignoring him, Hazel carefully knocked a full length ash from the cigarette she had lit, and crushed it out. Kate had not seen her smoke this cigarette, nor the one before it.

As the door closed behind Taylor, the overstuffed apartment seemed somehow less crowded. Kate asked bluntly, "Is there a particular reason why you dislike my partner, Hazel?"

"He's got big feet," she said, lighting another cigarette. "Can't abide men with great big feet. Never fails, the bigger the feet, the smaller the brain.

Lyndon Johnson had big feet. Look what a pea brain he was." She put the cigarette in the ashtray.

Kate smiled, thinking of the theory she had always heard about men with big hands and feet. "I guess I've heard stranger beliefs. But I can tell you it doesn't apply to Detective Taylor." Except sometimes, she added in inward amusement.

"Detective, you're a real good-looking woman when you smile. But then I guess you don't have much cause to smile in your line of work."

The white Persian cat sauntered into the room, cautiously sniffed the armchair she had been ousted from, and leaped onto the sofa beside Hazel. Hazel stroked her, the liver-spotted hand moving firmly through the long white fur. "Jerome now, he had such lovely feet, I used to buy him velvet maroon slippers . . ." The watery voice drifted off.

Sorry that she had to disturb Hazel's reverie, Kate said softly, "We understand Mr. Sinclair hadn't been feeling too well. Do you know anything about that?"

"He'd come down with some stomach miseries."

"Indigestion, you mean?"

"Worse, from what he said."

"Do you remember what he said?"

She lifted her hand from the cat's fur to gesture vaguely. "It was an uproar in his stomach, that's all. Nausea, he said. Sometimes he threw up, sometimes his nose and his skin felt funny to him. Sounded like allergy to me, probably to that stinking bourbon he drank — and that's what I told him."

"Do you know if he went to a doctor?"

"He started to lose some weight, and that's when

I told him to quit his whining and do something. Don't know if he did or not."

"Hazel, you mentioned that Mr. Sinclair didn't get on well with Mr. Parker or Mr. Crane. Can you tell me the nature of the disagreement?"

"Politics," Hazel said succinctly.

Using the tactic of silence, Kate continued to write in her notebook.

Hazel finally offered, "A lot of people in this building had trouble with Owen's politics."

"Why? What were his politics?"

She shrugged. "I don't pay attention to any of that business. Jerome got way deep into all that, but I never did. I don't like politics or politicians. The Democrats, they want to take from the useful people and give to the useless ones. The Republicans, they want to take what little bit poor folks manage to get and give it to people that are already so rich it's hideous. Now Reagan, he doesn't have big feet, so he came by his pea brain all by himself. Now Reagan —"

"Most people agree to disagree on politics," Kate interrupted, entertained but needing to conclude this interview. "Why did Mr. Sinclair's politics create animosity in the people here?"

"You'll just have to ask them, won't you," Hazel declared, and Kate knew that for the moment further questions in this area were useless.

Looking at the cigarette burning untouched in the ashtray, Kate said, "I have one more question, Hazel. It's just curiosity. Why do you light cigarettes and not smoke them?"

"I can't abide smoking, even lighting one of those things is like putting burnt feathers in my mouth.

Jerome was a chain-smoker, it's what killed him. Even so I missed the smell of it when he was gone. When people smoked in here it was like Jerome was back. So I went out and got some cigarettes for myself."

Kate nodded. "I understand perfectly," she said, and with effort said no more, did not — could not — share with Hazel that after Anne's death she had felt an almost crushing need to again take up smoking, but had resisted because of Anne's dislike of her old habit, the need to please Anne no different after her death than before.

Hazel seemed to shrink against the sofa. "I guess this . . . awful thing about Owen is partly on me, isn't it?"

"How so, Hazel?" Kate asked gently.

"I didn't do nothing about Owen and the people here that hated him, just let things fester. And I knew . . . I knew, you see. The first time I set eyes on him there was something in him I didn't like." She sat up and pointed an accusing finger at the urns. "You knew too, Jerome. You knew all about what I thought. It's your doing too, Jerome —"

Kate got up from the loveseat. "It's the doing of the person who took Mr. Sinclair's life from him. It's none of your doing at all, Hazel. Or Jerome's."

Hazel walked with Kate to the door. She took Kate's arm, pulled Kate down to her and kissed her cheek. "You're a dear good woman," she said.

– 4 –

As Kate emerged from the second floor staircase, she saw Aimee Grant in the hallway talking with Felix Knapp, the patrol officer assigned to safeguard the hallway and crime scene.

Aimee leaned against the wall near Paula Grant's apartment, her arms crossed, facing toward Kate. She looked somewhat disheveled: the white silk shirt had been pulled out to hang over the black pants, and the heavy dark hair had lost its smoothness, had separated into streams as if she had been running her fingers through it. She watched Kate come down the hall toward her.

Knapp, engrossed in Aimee Grant, finally noticed her diverted attention and turned around. Kate nodded to him. He straightened his broad young shoulders, then his gunbelt, and self-consciously strode off to again take up his post near the back stairway.

Kate said to Aimee, "You're free to leave if you wish. We'll have a statement for you to sign, maybe a few more questions — but we know where to reach you." The young woman seemed well recovered from her shock: the blue-violet eyes were alert and curious in their scrutiny of Kate's face.

"I'll be right here," Aimee said crisply. "My aunt's asleep but I'm staying with her. At least for the weekend."

Pleased that Aimee felt such strong protectiveness for Paula, Kate nodded and smiled. Taylor was right, she conceded; Aimee Grant was remarkably attractive. Aside from her youthful resilience and the fine eyes and glossy hair, there was vitality here, and intelligence, and a strong sensual presence.

"Good night, then," Kate said.

About to enter Owen Sinclair's apartment, Kate turned at the bidding of some instinct; Aimee Grant stood where Kate had left her, staring at her.

Taylor sat in Owen Sinclair's recliner making notes from the Field Investigation cards completed by Hansen's officers. Kate picked up the FI cards he had discarded, and took the armchair opposite him.

"Vivian Sinclair," he said, and heaved a sigh. "So stoned she talked like she had a shoe in her mouth. Pretty much said what Hazel told us, except she put it a little different to me."

Taylor flipped back several pages of his notebook, seeking a particular note. " 'I don't care a feeble fuck about the chickenshit asshole' — that's what the lady said. I asked her why, she says, 'Fuck off, I'm tired,' and drops the phone on the floor." He touched his ear, wincing. "What a night. A landlady from cloud cuckooland hauls out four jugs of her husband's ashes, then a foul-mouthed old bat breaks my eardrum with her phone."

Chuckling, Kate said mischievously, "Hazel Turner's nuts about your feet."

"Yeah?" He stretched out his legs and admired his brown wingtip shoes. "Really likes 'em, huh?"

"I didn't say she liked them, I said she was nuts about them."

Taylor laughed. "Good old Hazel. Kate, isn't there some kind of law in this state about proper ways you have to handle ashes after cremation?"

"Indeed there is," Kate said. "You want to do something about Jerome?"

Taylor held up both hands. "Who, me? I was just asking. Poor bastard, he can't rest in peace even when he's dead."

Grinning, Kate riffled through the FIs. "Anything stand out in these?"

"Not that I see, Kate." He handed her the rest of the cards. "It's late and a lot of people we want to talk to aren't kids."

Kate smiled at him. "You mean you don't want to pack up your three old lady suspects and haul them

56

in? It's only midnight after all, the station's only clear on the other side of the division."

He looked wounded. "Our killer *is* right here, Kate. What Hazel says about the keys, you gotta admit that. We got a lock on this case." She winced at the pun, and he grinned. "It's plain as the shoes on my feet how our killer just unlocked Sinclair's door and walked right in. Whoever did this ain't going nowhere, she'll be waiting for us tomorrow. So I say we button up and let everybody else in the place calm down and get some sleep; we can finish up that part of it tomorrow."

Some elements in the case were indeed clear, Kate reflected. From Paula Grant's statements about when Owen Sinclair arrived at the party and when he had left, and what Everson had disclosed about the delayed reaction of strychnine, the poison must have been administered at the party. If the killer had a key to Sinclair's apartment, the phone cord could have been cut beforehand, the poison might have been placed beforehand in Sinclair's bourbon. But that meant the killer had prior knowledge that Sinclair would bring his own bottle to the party . . .

She glanced at her watch, impatient to put more detail of this case together. But they had to finish processing the crime scene; it was imperative that they collect everything of any possible value to establish a continuity of evidence. If or when this case went to trial they could then prove conclusively that no outside tampering with the crime scene had been possible. And it *was* late — most of the tenants had undoubtedly gone to bed, whatever their age.

"I made a list," Taylor said. "There's the two other old ladies, Maxine Marlowe and Mildred Coates.

Cyril Crane and this Parker Thomas fellow, they argued with the victim at the party, maybe there's something there. We got Dudley Kincaid and Dorothy Brennan. Everybody else was outta here for the day, so they're low priority."

"So it appears," Kate said. She picked up the FIs. "I want to get my notes and my head in order." She glanced again at her watch: 11:58. She smiled. "Happy Thanksgiving."

He pulled his bulky body out of the recliner. "Yeah, sure," he said.

– 5 –

At five-thirty in the morning Kate picked up the *Los Angeles Times* outside her doorway and walked into her apartment. She turned on the lights, illuminating immaculate neatness except for a stack of magazines and six books scattered across the teak coffee table — bright, welcoming richness. Just last week she had borrowed the books, along with copies of *The Advocate,* from Joe D'Amico. Joe and Salvatore, his lover, were her source for information about the community of gay men she had come to regard as her brothers.

She had read through her latest lesbian books and passed them on to Maggie Schaeffer. While she waited for more, this collection would fill the void quite nicely.

Knowing she must give herself a break from the events of the past hours, she plugged in the coffee pot, then stripped off her clothing and walked into the shower, thinking about Maggie and Maggie's Nightwood Bar, and the lesbians she had come to know during her homicide investigation there. Afterward, she had quickly, eagerly read her way through the dilapidated collection of lesbian books on the bar's bookshelves, grumbling to Maggie about the old copyright dates as well as the considerable variation in literary quality.

"There's lots more books out there, damn good ones," Maggie had growled. "Every time I walk into Sisterhood Bookstore to pick up *The Lesbian News* I leave drool marks all over the shelves. Books are expensive, Kate. You can afford them, lots of us can't. Why don't you march in there and buy some for yourself and then donate them to the bar?"

Kate had risked becoming a regular at the Nightwood Bar, risked attending the annual Gay Pride Parade in West Hollywood — but at least these were somewhat circumscribed hazards because she was mainly within her own community. Maggie, who had been openly a lesbian since the age of thirteen, did not and could not understand that Kate's career dictated limits to her freedom: "So what if somebody sees you, finds out about you? You're better off than most of us — you're protected by city ordinance."

"That doesn't *matter*, Maggie," Kate had tried to explain. "We have over seven thousand police officers and nobody's out, not a soul. You can't begin to fathom the homophobia. My life would be hell, I wouldn't be able to function."

"There has to be an end to it, Kate," Maggie had answered her with quiet emphasis. "All of you staying in the closet will never ever put an end to it."

If Maggie challenged the necessity for caution and discretion, Joe D'Amico surely did not; he worked in the LAPD crime lab, and knew the same stories she did. Last month Mitch Grobeson, a former sergeant at Pacific Division who had compiled a superb performance record, had filed the first-ever lawsuit, claiming extreme harassment because he was homosexual, claiming endangerment to his life in the performance of his job — that he had been persecuted and tormented into resigning. Joe D'Amico understood as well as she did that LAPD's queer-hating fraternity of macho cops would turn a gay officer's existence into a nightmare. She did not want to become a Mitch Grobeson. Without a permanent relationship in her life, her work was more important to her now than ever.

And so she regularly gave Maggie money to buy lesbian books and periodicals which Maggie placed in the bar library after Kate had read them. Kate would have liked to keep some of the books on her own bookshelves for the warmth and close comfort of their company, but she had made an agreement with Maggie.

Toweling her hair, Kate walked into her living room and switched on the TV, needing to fill the silence that echoed through her rooms at this sepulchral hour of the morning. She was jolted by a panning shot of the exterior of the Beverly Malibu, a brief clip of Lieutenant Bodwin. Then the newscaster jovially said to stay tuned for a weather forecast and more news at sunrise.

She flipped open the *Times* and found two short paragraphs headlined WESTSIDE MURDER on page four of the Metro section. Life in the big city, Taylor would say. The death of another ant in the anthill. Well, she would uncover the ant who had turned into a killer ant and remove it from the hill.

Coffee in hand, she went to her closet, inspected her wardrobe. Today Paula Grant would see that she could wear clothing much more professional than a windbreaker and pants.

Paula Grant . . .

Why was this woman, so many years her senior, so very attractive to her? She was drawn by Paula Grant's strength qualities — and there was no precedent for it. She had always been attracted to a very different sort of woman, a woman with softer, more responsive attributes, like Anne, like Ellen O'Neill, like Andrea Ross . . .

Kate shrugged at herself in the mirror. What did it matter? At this point, since she did not seem emotionally equipped for casual sex, close platonic friendship with other lesbian women seemed a more likely future for her than the complete marriage she had shared with Anne.

She was recovering from Anne, but sexually she had been somehow spun into a cocoon. She had had two serious affairs, both unsuccessful, and since then had met women who interested her, but none who had awakened her. Until Paula Grant . . .

Instead of heading as usual toward the Santa Monica Freeway and Wilshire Division, Kate drove east on Montana Avenue. Traffic in the city of Santa Monica was almost nonexistent on this Friday after Thanksgiving, especially at the gray hour of six-thirty a.m.

She did not travel this direction on Montana that often; her customary path to and from home was limited to the western end of the street with its pricey cafes and upscale boutiques. She looked pleasurably through the gloom at neatly kept apartment buildings, and as the wide tree-lined street curved along the edge of Brentwood Country Club she rolled down her window and inhaled the cool moist green of the heavy foliage concealing the golf course. She remembered noting a Brentwood address on an FI: Aimee Grant lived near here.

She sped down Wilshire Boulevard beside the vast, impeccable greenery of the Veteran's Administration Hospital, and slowed at the Federal Building. Through the gray it looked like a tall white tombstone circled by flags. To her left, down quiet, eucalyptus-lined Veteran Avenue, lay real tombstones, cold gray-white and precisely aligned, row upon row and acre upon acre, some of the graves containing young men she had served with during her tour in Vietnam. She nodded in somber salute.

Imposing edifices now loomed over Wilshire

Boulevard: marble-faced office buildings, luxurious high-rise apartments studded with balconies. Not for the first time she marveled at the wealth in this enormous city, how so many people could have amassed so much money.

Wilshire intersected with Santa Monica Boulevard, and she drove alongside the posh Beverly Hills shopping district where Christmas decorations were already in evidence, the streets so devoid of their usual traffic and crowds of shoppers and tourists that the city appeared as lifeless as a ghost town. She glanced at the Moorish elegance of the police building on Rexford Drive, amused by its incongruous contrast to the modern brick bulk of her own Wilshire Division.

Two minutes later she parked the Plymouth across from the Beverly Malibu. Taylor's Caprice was parked in front of the building, engine ticking as it cooled.

The front door of the Beverly Malibu opened; Paula and Aimee Grant emerged, Aimee wearing the rumpled clothing of the day before. Paula, in a loose fitting gray sweater and a pair of perfectly pressed black chinos, pierced Kate with the delicate strength of her femininity. From the impassive glance Paula cast over her attire, Kate doubted that her camel-hair jacket and green gabardine pants, the best clothing she owned, impressed her.

Paula nodded greeting. "As we told Detective Taylor, I'm going for a walk," she informed Kate in her resonant tones.

"And I'm on my way home to pick up some clothes," Aimee said.

"Fine," Kate said, appreciating that the women

were conveying full cooperation with her investigation.

She watched Paula's graceful strides until she vanished from sight. Then she pressed the button beside Hazel Turner's name and announced herself, and was buzzed entry into the building.

Taylor sat at the table in the community room sipping coffee from one of two styrofoam cups, each the size of a megaphone. He pushed the other cup toward her.

"Thanks, Ed." She sat down and uncapped the huge container.

"Here, let me have that muck," Hazel Turner ordered from the doorway. Wearing an orange floral housecoat and green thongs, she flapped over to the table and wrested Kate's coffee from her. "You can't drink this. Gimme yours too," she said to Taylor. "God knows what they put in here." Holding the cups at contemptuous arm's length, she went flapping out of the community room.

"God knows what she'll put in hers," Taylor muttered. "Let's hope to Christ she's not our killer." Leaning back in his chair, he yawned. "Short night, it's gonna be a long day."

Kate nodded. Last night they had finished processing the crime scene, including the collection of all edibles and potables from Owen Sinclair's apartment, as well as plastic bags from the dumpster, one of the bags filled with party trash — all of this for toxicological evaluation by the lab. Then they had gone to the station to enter the preliminary reports that would eventually comprise an indexed Murder Book for this case. She and Taylor had returned to their respective homes only to shower and change clothes.

Hazel returned with two huge coffee mugs. Taylor took his, winked at Kate, clinked it against her mug. "Here's to luck, partner," he said, and took a swallow. "Ah, Hazel, I should only have coffee this good before I die."

"I grind the beans fresh," Hazel informed him.

Pulling a green urn from her pocket, she placed it in the center of the table between two ashtrays, and sat down with the detectives. "You're early birds," she said. "Most folks here aren't up yet. They wouldn't be up even if this wasn't a holiday weekend."

"Hazel," Taylor said flatly, "we aren't conducting this homicide investigation at the convenience of your tenants."

"Listen, mister smarty-pants cocky detective, you just try and talk to Maxine right now. Go ahead and break her door down — she still won't give a peep till ten o'clock. Takes her that long to get her warpaint on. Mildred, she's got arthritis bad, takes her a good long time these damp winter mornings to get the kinks out." She shook a finger at Taylor. "You want cooperation, sonny, you better listen to what Hazel here has to tell you. I know my building, I know my —"

"Of course," Kate said as Taylor took refuge in his coffee mug. She opened her notebook to the list of interviews Taylor had prioritized last night and placed an X beside Maxine Marlowe and Mildred Coates. "How about Mr. Crane?"

"He's up. He's an actor, he takes real good care of himself. He's already been out for his morning constitutional."

Kate placed a check mark beside Crane's name. "And Mr. Kincaid?"

"Dudley's one of those writer types," Hazel said, wrinkling her nose in disapproval. "Never can tell about him." She leaned over and gripped Kate's arm. "Honey, I been thinking about this, turning it all over in my head these last hours. I think it's him, Dudley."

"Why is that, Hazel?"

"Because I don't like him."

Kate said gently, "Surely there's another reason?"

"It's a good enough reason," Hazel contended. "I got real good instincts about not liking people."

Kate returned to her list, placing a check mark beside Dudley Kincaid. "How about Mr. Thomas?" She was interested as well as amused by Hazel's impressions of the tenants under suspicion.

"Parker Thomas, he's another writer type but if you ask me, he should of been a preacher. Looks like he walked right out of that picture of the Last Supper. He's up and around, always is around eight or so. And Dorothy Brennan, she'll be on her balcony or in the laundry room or somewhere. She's a busybody, too nosy by half, if you ask me."

Because she's encroaching on your territory, Kate thought, catching Taylor's grin and wink. She said to Hazel, "I didn't realize you had balconies. They're not visible from the street."

"There's only two. You can't see 'em, there's

shrubbery along the side that hides 'em. Dorothy's got one, Nancy Billington's got the other. Real small, just big enough for some plants and maybe a chair."

Taylor asked, "Could someone get in through those balconies?"

"Nope," Hazel said. "You'd need to truck a ladder around the side."

Kate had finished her coffee. She said to Taylor, "Ready?"

– 6 –

The young black man who answered Cyril Crane's door wore a powder blue sweatshirt cut off above the waist and at the elbows; still it hung from his shoulders in a huge shapeless mass. His jeans, faded to blue-white, were cinched by a wide belt tightened to its final notch.

"Cyril just hit the shower," the young man explained as he looked over Kate and Taylor's identification. "He'll be at least fifteen minutes. My name's Houston."

Kate, recognizing the name Doyle Houston from

the FIs, suspected that like Aimee Grant he had come here dressed for Thanksgiving without any intention of staying over, and had borrowed this ill-fitting costume from Cyril Crane.

"Fine," she said, entering the living room. "We need to talk to you as well, Mr. Houston." The apartment was permeated by a light, perfumy fragrance — from Cyril Crane's ablutions in the bathroom, she assumed.

"Houston, everybody calls me Houston. Do sit down, be comfortable. I'll be right back."

Taylor's silence drew a glance from her. He had hunched his shoulders and crossed his arms. Alerted by this hostile body language, she glanced around. On the walls were framed charcoal caricatures of Marilyn Monroe, Gloria Swanson, and Lana Turner — but his gaze had been drawn by a dominant photo of Rock Hudson. *Cyril, you're beautiful,* the inscription read, and was signed, *Rock.* Beside the photo, on an ivory-topped stand, knelt a large bronze male figure, his shoulders thrown back, his hips thrust forward in prideful display of his genitalia.

She was well aware that this evidence and the presence of black man Doyle Houston, not to mention the decidedly unmasculine fragrance in the apartment, had activated most of Taylor's not-so-latent prejudices. Equally plain documentation of women in Paula Grant's apartment had escaped his interpretation — but then his antenna always seemed more attuned to men. She gave a mental shrug. If he jeopardized the conduct of this interview, she would simply send him out of the apartment on another assignment.

Again she looked around. The living room seemed spacious and filled with light, a perception created by windows open to the day and by the pale colors of the furnishings. The off-white sofa, and the matching chairs in which she and Taylor seated themselves, had seen better days, as had the gold-edged white tables. The peach-hued, shell-like bases of twin table lamps looked expensive; they were as delicate and translucent as mother-of-pearl. The real colors in the room emanated from a grouping of oil paintings, modern art of striking red swirls and a complexity of green and blue shapes. She knew virtually nothing about art but suspected that these works were valuable objects in a shabby room in which area rugs did not quite conceal worn spots in the carpet.

Doyle Houston returned with a tray containing a coffee carafe, a pitcher of orange juice and a plate of apple Danish. "What can I serve you?" The voice was a light baritone.

"Nothing," Taylor said.

"I'd appreciate some orange juice," Kate said.

As he poured her a generous glassful, she studied him with interest. His hair was trimmed to no more than an inch in length and framed a high, wide forehead. The wide-apart almond-shaped eyes were an intense dark brown, the nose small and flared, the jaw-line square and firm, the face tight-fleshed except for sensuously shaped lips. She thought that his head would make a fine sculpture, that the burnished tones of his skin and the light blue colors of his clothing were beautiful in this bland room.

Houston, in stockinged feet, seated himself cross-legged on the sofa and poured himself a cup of coffee. "I don't know a thing," he said, "but ask away." The words were spoken with precision; his faint smile contained a hint of cynicism.

Kate asked, "When did you and Mr. Crane go to the party yesterday?"

"Party? A party is something you're supposed to enjoy," Houston said. "We went down around one-thirty or so."

Kate was remembering Hazel Turner's characterization of him as "smart alecky." Was it racial prejudice? Or something substantive? She asked, "Why didn't you enjoy it?"

He shrugged. "Maybe my mood. These days I find Thanksgiving a little depressing around the edges. Maxine Marlowe's usually fun, but not when she's bored. I get a kick out of Hazel the landlady — anybody who thinks *The Diary of Anne Frank* is the best book ever written can't be all bad. But she was too busy being hostess. So Aimee and I watched TV."

"When did you leave the party?"

"I'd guess around three. There was some sort of intermission in the football game."

Taylor said condescendingly, "I take it you're not much of a football fan."

Houston looked at him frankly. "I must confess I find sports rather stupid. Aimee did her best to educate me, and I did enjoy watching the athletes."

Kate inquired, "While you were watching TV, what did Mr. Crane do?"

He picked up his coffee cup and gestured vaguely with it. "Oh . . . he was . . . circulating."

"You seem to know the other tenants quite well," Kate observed, backing away for the moment from the topic of Cyril Crane's activities at the party.

Houston visibly relaxed. "Cyril and I've been friends for years. I know most of his neighbors pretty well."

"Including Mr. Sinclair?"

"Not him."

"Why not?"

"Ask Cyril. He lives here."

"We understand there was an argument between Mr. Crane and Mr. Sinclair at the party."

"Argument? There was some kind of discussion involving a number of people, including Cyril. I didn't listen to what was being said."

She knew she would elicit no further information from him on this point. "Did you happen to notice anything Mr. Sinclair ate or drank?"

"I saw him come in with his bourbon bottle under his arm, which I thought was disgusting. Other than that, he isn't the type I'd ever pay a second's attention to."

"Who *is* the type?" said a cheerful voice from the hallway.

Cyril Crane strode into the room, his broad-shouldered, six-foot frame clad in a red sweatshirt and gray cotton drawstring pants. Soft white hair was combed casually back from a heavily tanned square face of timeless good looks — a finely shaped aquiline nose, wide and expressive lips, azure eyes. Only the folds of flesh around his mouth and under his eyes and chin revealed advanced maturity.

Kate introduced herself and Taylor. Taylor, his arms again folded, nodded stiffly. Crane returned Taylor's nod.

"Mr. Crane," Kate said, "would you give us a few more minutes with Houston? Then we'd like to talk to you."

He shrugged acquiescence. "I'll be in the back bedroom," he said to Houston.

Kate asked Houston, "What can you tell us about what happened last night?"

"Not very much. We were going over to a friend's house for dinner at eight o'clock, we were talking, watching television in the meantime. We heard screams from the hallway. We ran out, it was Aimee, Paula's niece, running down the hallway. Then Paula came out of Sinclair's place, said something terrible had happened to him. That's it."

"We understand there was some bad feeling between Mr. Sinclair and Paula Grant, Maxine Marlowe, and Mildred Coates. Do you know anything about that?"

"Only that they took a lot of abuse from him. Especially Max —" He broke off.

Kate pursued him. "Why Maxine?"

He looked distressed. "Nothing, I don't know anything at all. Just forget what I said."

"We can't forget anything that pertains to a homicide investigation. What about Maxine?"

"Nothing," he insisted, "I'm not saying anything about what I don't know anything about."

"Let me take a guess," Taylor said. "Maxine had some history with Sinclair, right? One of his plow jobs, right?"

Houston looked at him. "Are you always this crude?"

"I'm a cop doing my job," Taylor snapped, "not a —" He broke off.

"Sissy hair dresser?" Houston suggested mildly. "Interior decorator? Dress designer?"

"Houston," Kate intervened, "please answer the question."

"I already have. Anything you want to know

about Maxine, ask her yourselves." He got up from the sofa. "I've told you everything I know. I'll get Cyril." And he stalked from the room.

Taylor looked at Kate and shrugged contemptuously.

Cyril Crane walked into the room and sat on the sofa. Hunching over, his elbows on his thighs, his fingers steepled together, he peered up at Kate and Taylor and inquired in a mellifluous bass voice, "How can I help you detectives?"

Kate said courteously, "We understand you're an actor."

"These days only when old friends think of me," he said with a self-deprecating smile. He sat up and pulled a pack of Marlboros from the breast pocket of his sweatshirt. "I have a dear friend on *Murder, She Wrote*. I appeared several weeks ago."

"Hey, yeah, I remember," Taylor interjected with an animation that startled Kate. Chuckling, he said, "You were in that fancy restaurant, you were the Frenchman in the tux that applied the Heimlich maneuver when the guy choked."

Crane smiled charmingly. "Didn't do much good, did it?"

Taylor chuckled again. "The Heimlich maneuver never works on cyanide."

Watching Taylor, Kate marveled at how an appearance on a TV or movie screen could instantly transform someone in another person's eyes, make him into a figure perceived altogether differently.

Crane lit a Marlboro with a tall silver lighter, exhaling smoke in a thin stream. "The TV news says Sinclair was poisoned — a rather ghoulish coincidence. Was it cyanide as well?"

Taylor said, "We're not at liberty to say." His voice had reacquired some of its formality; Kate guessed that Crane was not sufficiently transformed to win Taylor's full approval. "Tell us what you know about what happened here yesterday."

"Not much to tell," Crane said easily. He poured two cups of coffee and handed one to Taylor, who hesitated, then accepted it.

"Mr. Crane," Kate said, "how long have you lived here?"

Crane drew again from his cigarette, handling it with a dexterous sophistication Kate recalled from movies of her youth. Paula Grant, she remembered, had smoked with equal elegance. Crane said, "I do believe it's been more than twenty-five years."

"I take it you were well acquainted with Mr. Sinclair?"

"Well enough."

"Were you friends?"

He looked coolly at Kate. "That's a very short list and I was never on it."

"Why is that, Mr. Crane?"

"I didn't like the things he did to people."

"Such as?"

He picked up his coffee and sipped from it, blowing on it between sips.

Kate finally decided that he was not going to answer. She said, "Did he do something to you?"

He put the cup back on the table. "Not to me personally. I could afford to dislike him purely on my own."

"We understand his loud music was . . . bothersome. Did it bother you?"

"Not unless I was in the hallway. I did what I

could for Paula, Mildred and Maxine — including an offer to buy him earphones. He claimed the sound wasn't the same except from his speakers. The truth is, the old bastard couldn't find women willing to put up with his abuse anymore, so he took it out on those three."

Taylor said, "We understand there was real trouble about that. Especially with Maxine."

Crane said, "Go ask the women about it yourselves. Owen Sinclair's no loss to this world. Even you'd want to mash a cockroach if you found one in your cupboard."

Kate said with some ire, "It's a bit more than mashing a cockroach, Mr. Crane. Someone took a human life in the most inhuman sort of way."

"You're presuming that the man in question was human."

Kate looked at him. He stared icily back at her. She said, "Besides the loud music, what other things did Mr. Sinclair do to people that caused you to despise him?"

Crane's smile was without warmth. "Most people feel that sometime in their lives they'd like to contribute to something larger than themselves. Owen Sinclair never thought anything was larger than himself."

Frustrated by Crane's evasiveness, Kate began to ask another question, but Taylor said, "You don't seem very worried about being a murder suspect."

"At this point in my life, Detective Taylor, I don't worry about much of anything. So I'm a suspect, am I?" He smiled.

Kate took another tack. "Do you know of anyone else who was an enemy of Mr. Sinclair's?"

"Enemy enough to kill him? Nobody in this building."

"Mr. Crane, the party yesterday — did you notice when Mr. Sinclair left?"

"I'm not sure," he said after a moment. "Before Houston and I did, which was around three or so. He left maybe five or ten minutes earlier. Actually, I think he was the first person to leave. Said he wasn't feeling well." Again he stared at Kate, his blue eyes widening as if he suddenly realized the significance of his words.

"What can you tell us about what happened last night?"

As Crane related hearing Aimee Grant's screams from the hallway, and the aftermath, Kate turned back to her notes of the interview with Houston and followed them, noting the identical sequence of events.

Kate said, "We understand Mr. Sinclair was a movie director. Did you ever work for him as an actor?"

"Work for *him*? Sinclair did nothing but trash. At my lowest ebb I would never stoop to — In my prime, my dear," Crane said, "I worked with real talent. I worked for Cukor. With James Whale on the classic *Frankenstein,* on the original *Showboat.* I —"

He suddenly smiled. "Houston was the one Sinclair approached about acting. And Houston's never acted before in his life." He slid an arm along the back of the sofa as if Houston were sitting there, a symbolic gesture that seemed both affectionate and protective.

"It was a few years back," Crane said with a grin. "He showed Houston two scripts with a total of four pages of dialogue. The titles were *Around the World in Sixty-Nine Ways* and *King Dong.*"

He laughed along with Kate and Taylor. Taylor asked, "Is that the kind of crap Sinclair directed?"

"In all fairness I don't know that he ever directed that kind of crap at all," Crane said. "I think he was mooching on the edges trying to make a few bucks. He never was very fussy about what he did for money."

He removed his arm from the sofa back and neatly extinguished his cigarette. "The late thirties, that was his peak. His specialty was western shoot-'em-ups. Believe it or not, the industry was putting out something like five thousand movies a year back then. This town was a factory, directors literally made up the stories as the camera rolled. But times changed. Audiences got a lot fussier, TV came in, movie westerns went out and stayed out. He tried TV, he tried theater, everybody threw him out. He blamed everything and everybody but himself. He had no talent of any kind — I've seen his movies and the plays he tried to write. Those TV lights and cameras here last night — he'd have been overjoyed."

Kate said, "Mr. Crane, we understand that you and the victim argued yesterday at the party."

Crane shrugged. "That. Oh, sure."

"Would you tell us what that was about?"

"Dorothy Brennan opened up some old wounds. The Beverly Malibu's claim to fame — I'm sure you know about it."

Kate was careful not to look at Taylor. "Why don't you tell us about it?"

"She dredged up HUAC."

"HUAC," Kate repeated, puzzled.

"Sorry, we've always used the acronym as a word. The House Un-American Activities Committee. In nineteen fifty-two, Owen Sinclair was a . . ." He sucked in his breath. "A . . . *friendly witness.*" The words were spoken with pure venom. "He named some of his friends and all of his enemies to the Committee. For years we've had a real live stool pigeon right here in our midst. And as usual Parker Thomas tried to find those non-existent brains of Sinclair's and make him hear exactly what he'd done."

"Mr. Crane," Kate said, "was yours a name Mr. Sinclair gave to the Committee?"

"No. I didn't even know him then. But he did name two acquaintances of mine. Who themselves went on to be informers, and spread the tragedy — they had no choice, they didn't have even the most minimal access to laws protecting other Americans."

He held up a hand to forestall Kate's next question. "Don't bother, I'll explain. They were gay men, prominent in the industry, and the FBI had compiled dossiers. Sexual dossiers, in addition to a political one about their connections to liberal causes. You can't imagine what it was like in the fifties, Detective Delafield, you were too young. To be accused of being a communist was one thing. To be threatened with exposure as a homosexual was to open the gates of hell. These two men became FBI informers, they had no other way to survive."

Taylor asked, "Who are the two men?"

"Under no circumstances will I ever give their names to anyone."

Kate said, "Mr. Crane, they may be involved in this."

"They're dead. They killed themselves. They've been dead for thirty years."

Taylor said, "Then what difference does it make if you tell us?"

"It makes no difference at all," Crane said. "Except to me."

Kate looked at him with respect. But she said, "We have only your word for it that they're dead."

"Get a list of the people Sinclair betrayed from the record of the hearings. Check everybody out for yourself."

"We'll indeed get the list. You say Dorothy Brennan opened this old wound. Why would she do that?"

He shrugged. "Curiosity. Anybody around Dorothy's age remembers those times very well. The young people who move in here — they think the world was invented yesterday. Except Parker Thomas, he's a younger man but he's involved in all sorts of historical research, so he knows. Dorothy asked me about Sinclair one time in the laundry room. Wanted to know if it was true he felt no qualms about what he'd done. She was quite fascinated, she —"

"Mr. Crane," Kate said, "at least tell us this much about the list of names given to that House Committee by the victim —"

"Victim," Crane repeated. "Sinclair is himself finally a victim. How wonderfully ironic."

"About the list," Kate said. "Is the name of any tenant in this building on it?"

"On Sinclair's list? No."

She looked down at her notebook, wanting to somehow corner this man and pull out the facts buried within him. Paula Grant probably had the same information as Cyril Crane, but she had shown every indication of being equally circumspect.

What she herself remembered about those historical events was sketchy. Senator Joseph McCarthy and Roy Cohn, and Lillian Hellman's defiance: *I cannot and will not cut my conscience to fit this year's fashions.* But she knew only these few surface facts and only from a distance; she had been eight years old during the Army-McCarthy hearings in 1954 and the final days of the anti-communist witch hunts. That time seemed far in the past, its repercussions entirely removed from this investigation.

"That's all I know," Crane said.

"We thank you," Kate said, rising. "Both you and Houston. We may have other questions. We'll be in touch."

Crane got up and extended a hand to Taylor. "Thank you for recognizing me. It's a compliment this old actor receives very rarely these days."

Taylor took his hand and shook it. "Sure," he said.

– 7 –

Mildred Coates answered her door after three knocks and a lengthy ringing of her doorbell. Patting yellowed gray hair pinned into a shapeless mass behind her head, she peered at Kate and Taylor's identification through thick glasses with heavy black frames. "Yes, all right," she murmured, and stepped back from the doorway.

This end apartment on the first floor was small and oppressively warm, yet Mildred Coates wore a wool skirt and a cardigan buttoned up to her throat. "May I get you some tea or coffee," she offered.

Taylor demurred, as did Kate, who was unbuttoning her jacket which she could not take off because her shoulder holster would be revealed. She hoped she would not perspire into her best clothing in this sweltering apartment. She knew that Taylor, who wore his weapon on his hip, would not remove his own jacket simply because he felt too deep-seated a sense of propriety around older women.

Mildred Coates lowered herself gingerly into the room's only armchair which faced a television set only a few feet away. Kate and Taylor settled themselves on the sofa. Dark blue drapes were drawn across the windows; a pole lamp behind a slip-covered sofa provided all of the room's dim light. Cheap bookshelves, crammed with paperbacks and a few unjacketed hardcovers, occupied the lower half of two otherwise barren walls. The living room reeked of cigarette smoke.

Kate's glance fell on Mildred Coates' left hand, which bore on its ring finger a wide gold band and a slim silver band with a tiny diamond. "Mrs. Coates —" she began.

"Indeed. Mrs. Andrew Coates. I don't believe in this Ms. business. Capable women can do plenty well enough in a man's world without all this foolishness about changing the language." The voice was querulous. "You look very capable," she told Kate. "I don't imagine you needed a bit of help getting to where you wanted. I never did get to where I wanted in my life, but it wasn't chauvinist men that stopped me."

Kate occupied herself with extracting a different pen from her shoulder bag, knowing it was useless to mention the legal pressure on the police hierarchy during the 1970s that made possible her presence in this room today. Clearly, Taylor would be more effective than she in interviewing Mildred Coates, and Kate nodded to him.

"Ma'am," he said, "would you tell us what you know about what happened here yesterday?"

"I don't know anything at all. I didn't even know anything *had* happened till I heard all the commotion, the sirens, the police coming in."

Kate studied her. The magnified dark eyes behind the thick lenses were perceptive, wary, resentful. Since this apartment was directly below that of Owen Sinclair, it was imperative that Taylor carefully and thoroughly elicit information from her.

He asked, "What time did you arrive at the party?"

"The invitation was for one o'clock," she said sharply. "I don't believe in this fashionably late business. One o'clock's when I arrived."

"And Mr. Sinclair, do you remember when he arrived?"

"Fashionably late. I don't know exactly when, I don't have a watch. He came in with Maxine Marlowe, her looking like a tart as usual, him with that bourbon bottle under his arm and wearing a sport shirt like Thanksgiving was just any ordinary day."

"Did you notice anything about Mr. Sinclair during the party, did you see anything that looked . . . strange about him?"

"I didn't pay one bit of attention to him. I talked to Parker Thomas, and Paula Grant and Dorothy Brennan. Especially Dorothy — she's been very kind to me. I don't know about the young people today and all their drugs, but Paula's niece and that young black friend of Cyril's were decently dressed and polite, even if their watching television was a bit rude. But I don't blame them for not wanting to put up with old fogies like ourselves."

Taylor dutifully smiled. "When did you go back to your apartment, ma'am?"

"Oh," she said, her eyes becoming remote, "I don't remember . . . the party seemed to break up all at once."

"After the party, when you were here in your apartment, did you hear anything out of the ordinary?"

"Hear anything? Out of the ordinary?" She looked at him in puzzlement.

"From Mr. Sinclair's apartment," he said patiently. "We understand his loud music was very bothersome to you. Isn't that so?"

"Well, in a manner of speaking, but . . ." She touched the side of her thick-framed glasses. "I wear a hearing aid. And I just turn it off, you see. I don't need it to hear the two things that matter — the ring of the telephone and the doorbell."

Kate almost laughed at Taylor's discomfiture; so much for Mildred Coates as a possible suspect for his loud-music-as-torture theory.

Taylor persisted, "Didn't you once call the police because of his music?"

"That was my grandniece. She was here and heard it, you see, and insisted he turn it down and when he wouldn't she got so terribly angry . . ."

Mildred Coates lit a Winston, and coughed, drew in more smoke, and coughed again. Kate sighed. The

Beverly Malibu, with all of its smokers, could create its own smog alert.

"It was never the music, really," Mildred Coates said. "Just the vibration, the humming from those great big speakers. So I'd turn off my hearing aid. I could still feel the vibration, but without the music it didn't bother me so much. And when the vibration stopped it was fine . . ."

"But it *did* bother you," Taylor coaxed, "having to do that all the time. It must have."

"Oh," she said vaguely, "you get used to it. You do, you know. I was a motion picture editor in my day, and to tell the truth I'm quite a movie watcher. I often sleep all day so I can watch the late-lates. That's when many really fine films are on, uncut. I'm a great reader, too." She picked up a large magnifying glass from the table beside her and gestured to the crowded bookcases. "I've collected many wonderful books, they're like old friends I visit often."

"We understand Paula Grant was a script supervisor," said Kate. "You must have a lot in common."

"Indeed we do." Her smile was fleeting, sweet and sad. "We worked together on *Easy Come, Easy Go,* a gangster picture in nineteen forty-nine with — well, you wouldn't know the actors, you're both too young. Believe it or not, I had a chance at quite a career as a film editor." She took off her glasses, polished a corner of a lens with her skirt.

Without the glasses the old face looked smaller to Kate, and pitiably vulnerable. Taylor, Kate saw, was content for the moment to let the old woman talk.

"When you edit a motion picture," Mildred Coates said, "you sit for long tedious hours in a dark little room. You take thousands of feet of raw footage through two rough cuts, through negative print, sound mix and looping and color timing — until finally you have your answer print. I loved every step of that way. But my eyes went on me, began to hemorrhage from the strain. I so wish . . ." She put on her glasses and pulled her cardigan higher around her throat. "Dorothy Arzner taught me how to edit. Did Paula by chance mention her?"

"She did, yes," Kate answered gently.

She nodded. "Dorothy Arzner was a remarkable woman. Did you know she edited *Blood and Sand*? Nineteen twenty-two it was, at Paramount. Imagine, a woman doing that back in nineteen twenty-two. I met her ten years later, when I was twenty. I was assistant cutter on two of her pictures, and from there I went on to be editor on many other pictures over the next twenty years. Until nineteen fifty-two, and then everything in the world fell apart."

Kate did some rapid math; Mildred Coates was seventy-six years old.

Mildred Coates puffed again on her cigarette, and again coughed. "You see, my husband was a member of the Communist Party for a brief time. I wasn't a bit interested in his politics, but I didn't see the harm in what he did. But in nineteen-fifty the FBI came for him."

Watching the calm old face, Kate listened intently, thinking that neither Paula Grant nor Hazel Turner nor Cyril Crane had chosen to reveal what they surely had known about Mildred Coates.

"You can't imagine what it was like to find out

they were watching us, had been for years. Perfect strangers knew all about us, everything, every small detail about our lives was written down in a file for complete strangers to poke into. Andrew, he'd joined the Party in nineteen thirty-four, you see, for the same reasons a lot of people did in those days. Not for lacking love for this country but believing it should be a better place than the one that brought on a Depression and financial ruination to our families and everyone we loved. When it was plain what Communism was all about, Andrew quit the Party."

The magnified dark eyes had clouded as they looked down the corridor of the years. "The FBI, they wanted him to testify — to identify everybody he knew. They already had the names. But he wouldn't do it. And then a man we thought was a friend named Andrew to the Committee in Washington. And that was the end of it. Andrew's name was picked up by the American Legion and all the anti-Communist publications in the country. He lost his real estate job. Jack Warner himself saw to it that I got fired. I couldn't get editing work anywhere. You can't begin to imagine . . . Then Andrew smashed our Oldsmobile into a tree and died."

Again she puff-coughed her cigarette. "Friends, relatives — they'd long since abandoned us. Except for Jerome Turner. It was nineteen fifty-three, the Beverly Malibu was brand new then. Jerome was good enough to welcome me. Some wonderful Jewish people he knew gave me a job in their carpet company. And then in nineteen sixty-seven a woman who wrote musicals for MGM, she'd given names to the Committee to her everlasting regret, she found out about me and pulled strings to get me back into editing . . ." She trailed off, absorbed in her memories.

Taylor asked with quiet care, "Did you know about Mr. Sinclair's testimony to the House Un-American Activities Committee?"

Mildred Coates shifted in her armchair and extinguished her cigarette. "He was a . . . friendly witness." She uttered the words with difficulty. "He was . . . an informer."

"How did you feel about that, ma'am?"

Through the thick lenses, the dark eyes moistened as they contemplated Taylor. Kate, anguished by what she was witnessing in this tiny, oppressive apartment, knew that Taylor was asking exactly the right questions, the necessary questions.

"Down through all these years I've thought about it," Mildred Coates answered. "In the beginning, when I was so sick with grief, I wished Andrew had done the same thing as Owen. I thought it would have kept him alive, you see. But he'd have despised himself too much to go on living on this earth, he'd have died in a worse agony. Mostly I've wished he'd stood by his decision not to cooperate and just let us get through it as best we could until the witch hunting stopped, you knew that the decent people in this country would finally put an end to it. But instead he did the one thing that couldn't ever be changed — he took himself away from me, he left me all alone."

"Ma'am," Taylor asked softly, "was it Mr. Sinclair who named your husband?"

She stared at him. "Why, he didn't even know Andrew."

Taylor paused, to write briefly in his notebook. "Still — didn't you feel bitterness toward Mr. Sinclair for appearing before that Committee? For being an informer?"

"Bitterness." Mildred Coates pursed her lips and gazed fixedly before her, as if the word were written in the air. "Let me explain to you," she said.

Again she took off her glasses, and leaned back in her armchair and closed her eyes. "If I could just have had those years I lost to the blacklist. I know I could have been a great editor. I know I could have been Verna Fields, I could have been Dede Allan. The other night I saw *Bonnie and Clyde* again, all those ground-breaking quick cuts Dede Allan made on that picture. I was already integrating some of those techniques. I could have been the first really great woman editor . . ."

She put on her glasses and pointed to the blank television screen. "I look at movies from the time I couldn't work, and know what I could have done with them."

Kate's pen had long since stilled over her notes. She understood why, unlike the apartments of Paula Grant and Cyril Crane, there was no prideful evidence of Mildred Coates' profession anywhere in this room. This murder investigation now seemed to be inflicting cruelties on the living, disturbing too many memories better left dormant in the rooms and halls of the Beverly Malibu.

"My grandniece thinks Andrew was a hero," Mrs. Coates said. "She moved here a year ago, she's got a job at MGM. Her life will be so different from mine . . ."

She said to Taylor, "You want to how I felt about

Owen Sinclair. He was an informer. Alive or dead, that's what he was and that's what he'll always be — an informer."

Her gaze took in both Kate and Taylor. Her voice had strengthened. "My grandniece is right, Andrew *is* a hero. I'm Mrs. Andrew Coates, wife of a man who refused to get down on his knees for his politics and wouldn't name the names of people who were his friends. I'll die being proud of that."

Kate closed her notebook and picked up her shoulder bag.

Mildred Coates struggled to her feet. "You've been very courteous, both of you." She said to Kate, "It's good to have a woman doing this job. Those FBI men in their dark suits — you just knew they could shoot you dead at their feet and never give another thought to it. Do you know if they have women in the FBI now?"

"Yes, Mrs. Coates," Kate said. "They have a few."

– 8 –

Maxine Marlowe wore an emerald-green skirt and a black V-neck blouse. A round gold pendant hung within the V, just above the cleavage of abundant breasts whose tops were visibly puffed up by rigid corseting. Above the pendant, half a dozen other gold chains encircled tanned flesh laced with fine wrinkles.

Waving away the identification Kate and Taylor extended, heaving a sigh, Maxine Marlowe granted entrance to her apartment. Kate caught the floral-acid odor of gin on her breath.

As Kate walked through the doorway, a huge oil painting of a young Maxine Marlowe, her breasts bulging from a strapless red evening gown, stared from across the room, the baby mouth in a seductive pout. The entire living room was a mirror reflection of the actress: photos and movie posters of her decorated every inch of every wall.

Her hips swaying, a powerful aroma of perfume in her trail, she led the detectives across discolored white carpeting to a tattered sectional sofa of red velvet cushions. Taylor walked over to a wall of photographs. Kate sat down and immediately sank into pillowing as treacherous as quicksand. While she struggled to maintain some sort of erect posture, Maxine Marlowe seated herself in a wing chair of faded gold satin, picked up a drink from one of three white lacquered chow tables, and complacently watched Taylor.

Managing to brace herself somewhat, Kate appraised the actress. She wondered if the white-blonde hair curled artfully over the plump shoulders was a wig; it appeared identical to the tresses in the oil painting and the photos. But makeup and powder now caked the folds and wrinkles of an aged face. The brown eyes were thickly rimmed with black eyeliner and coated with green eyeshadow. Vivid lipstick had sunk into countless vertical crevices around a mouth that was no longer a baby mouth; it looked like a blood-red centipede.

Kate looked away to the black and white posters on the wall, where the youthful Maxine Marlowe was a bright-eyed, sassy-looking flirt in colonial days costume; a coy Elizabethan wench; a sultry gangster's moll; a dance hall girl luring a cowboy through the batwing doors of a western saloon. In one series of photos she lay provocatively on the deck of a boat in a bathing suit; in another she cast suggestive looks from under an immense hat. There were photos of her with John Wayne, William Powell, Charles Boyer, John Hodiak, Gig Young, Alan Ladd. Only one photo showed her with another woman, a drooping, bleary-eyed Tallulah Bankhead who held a champagne glass up to the camera, an arm around Maxine Marlowe seemingly more in support of herself than friendship with Marlowe.

"I've got more I can show you in the bedroom," the actress cooed to Taylor, and chuckled at his uncertain grin.

The room reeked of her perfume, a high sweet odor so cloying that Kate tried to take quick shallow breaths to prevent herself from coughing. With relief she saw Maxine Marlowe reach to the chow table for a cigarette; she would be thankful to breathe the smell of smoke.

Taylor was immersed in the photographs. "You knew a lot of famous people."

"*Knew* is the right word." The raspiness in the stentorian voice conveyed decades of heavy smoking and hard drinking. "Here's to old days, good days." She held up her drink and sipped. "The best days in this town. The Coconut Grove, Ciro's, the Mocambo, the King Cole Trio at the Trocadero — there's never been a time like that before or since."

"Miss Marlowe," Kate said. She knew that one addressed movie stars as "Miss," even movie stars one had never heard of.

The brown eyes swung to her. Through the makeup they were disapproving, as if contemplating an inconvenient nuisance. "I know shit about this. I only live here." The actress pulled smoke from her cigarette, sucking it in as if she would draw the cigarette fully into that wrinkled red maw.

Kate concentrated on looking steadily at her. "How long have you known Mr. Sinclair?"

"Too long." She placed the cigarette, a greasy red smear on its filter, on a chipped marble ashtray.

"How long, Miss Marlowe?" Kate persisted politely, even as dislike became a welling intensity within her.

A shrug. "Owen and me, we go back a long way." She picked up her cigarette. "I've lived here twenty years, sweetheart."

Kate resented the actress's familiarity, her disdain. "When did —" A pillow shifted, and the insidious sofa again drew her into its depths. Maxine Marlowe snickered. Furious, Kate struggled to right herself.

Taylor asked, "You ever work for him?" He had propped himself safely against an arm of the sectional.

A contemptuous flick of ash was her immediate answer. "Busby discovered me. Busby Berkeley. L. B. Mayer was *real* fond of me, honey. But I signed a long-term contract." Again she flicked ash. "I wasn't the only fool. Olivia and Bette fought their way out of it, but me —"

"You mean Olivia De Haviland and Bette Davis?" Taylor interrupted, gazing at her.

"Who else? I didn't have their clout, and I paid for it. They tossed me on the scrap heap, they loaned me out, I ended up in dogs nobody's ever heard of. Oh, I was in some good ones, *The Scoundrel, Idiot's*

Delight —" She rattled off a series of film titles unfamiliar to Kate. Taylor was nodding and grinning. Kate had never suspected his familiarity with old movies.

"But you gotta look real hard to find me," the actress said. Her laughter contained the rich easiness of someone who had come fully to terms with her past. "I had one hell of a lot of fun. And no, I never worked in any of Owen's rotten pictures."

"I swear I saw you on TV." Taylor leaned toward her, as if trying to translate her ample figure to the down-sizing of a TV screen. "Maybe a month ago. It was about these mobs of screeching vampires, it was some old horror —" He broke off in embarrassment.

She shrugged. "Yeah, I did a lot of slice and dice. And giant crickets that ate Pittsburgh, all that kind of shit. These days there's a million roles for women. Back in the old days, when this town decided you were too old —" She snapped her red-tipped fingers. "That was that. And I sure as hell could never play anybody's mother. So I did horror stuff, it kept me eating."

And this sofa, Kate thought sourly, having once more worked herself free of its mushy tentacles, must be a prop from one of those movies. She wanted to follow up on Marlowe's relationship with Sinclair, but decided to come back to it later. "What time did you arrive at the party yesterday, Miss Marlowe?"

"Sweetheart, that silly picnic was no party." The smile was indulgent. "I came down around one-thirty."

"Did you notice what time Mr. Sinclair arrived?"

"We made our grand entrance together."

"Was that planned?"

"Are you kidding?" Gripping her cigarette between long crimson nails, she crushed it out.

"Why would we be kidding?"

The actress shrugged.

"Did you notice what time he left?"

"Nope. I was outta there before anybody else."

"Why was that, Miss Marlowe?"

"It was a big fat bore. Owen and Parker and Dudley and Cyril were arguing. And there was a loud stupid football game on television. So I left."

"About what time was that?"

"Maybe two-thirty, quarter to three."

So Maxine Marlowe had "dropped in" for more than an hour. "What was the argument about?"

She shrugged. "The usual crap, and I'm sure you know all about it by now. There's a truce about the blacklist in this building, but that fool Dorothy Brennan brought it up again."

Kate said, "We take it there's animosity connected with this issue."

"An-i-mos-i-ty," the actress repeated, ticking off the five syllables on her fingers. "Like Paul Newman saying *mendacity* in *Cat on a Hot Tin Roof,* except he was pretty." The heavily madeup eyes had become stony in their contemplation of Kate. "It figures. Any woman that wants to be a cop figures to be a tight-ass. Trust a tight-ass lady cop to come up with *animosity* instead of a nice simple word like *hurt* or *hate.*"

Ambushed by this sudden hostility, Kate struggled to contain her flaring outrage.

"Miss Marlowe," Taylor said, "answer the question."

Maxine Marlowe addressed the fuming Kate. "Sweetheart, the blacklist hurt everybody. It mashed Mildred like a caterpillar. It hurt Paula, it hurt everybody here one way or the other. Yeah, sweetheart, there was *animosity*."

Kate stared back with equal stoniness. The actress was seizing on anything to belittle her. Her own best weapon was poise. But she had heard the comment about Paula. She made a note and circled it, then asked in a calm tone, "Did the investigation have any effect on your career?"

"Mine? Shit no. Commies, right wingers, I still got rotten parts. All of 'em screwed me." She chuckled. "And sometimes vice versa."

Taylor, leaning forward from where he was perched on the arm of the sofa, his ankles crossed, was assiduously making notes. Kate knew that this septuagenarian actress, with her propped up cleavage and her clown-like makeup and her coarseness, acutely offended him.

Kate asked, "What did you think about Mr. Sinclair's appearance before the Committee?"

"He didn't appear before the Committee. Only hot shit people got to do that. He was too small time, they only wanted big names, people good for headlines. He shot off his wad in closed session."

"Was Mr. Sinclair a Communist?"

"*Owen?*" Her laughter was harsh. "To be a Commie you gotta give a passing thought to politics. Owen never gave a shit about anything except boozing and screwing anybody he could. He hung around a few Party meetings, but even Commies wouldn't help a no-talent like him get a job."

Maxine Marlowe's perfume was again inundating

Kate; with relief she watched the actress light another cigarette.

"Owen thought wrapping himself in the flag would make him new friends, get him a good job in this town. Some of the biggest names in Hollywood — people like John Wayne and Irene Dunne, and Disney and Cooper and Gable and Stanwyck — they were saying it was just swell for the Committee to tell us who wasn't a real true-blue American. Adolphe Menjou got right down on his knees and licked their boots. Jack Warner said it was wonderful they were snooping under all our beds. L. B. was real cordial, too. The difference was, L. B. and Jack Warner didn't name names, none of those people did. Owen didn't have anything to give them *except* names, and he never did figure out why a lot of people thought that made him an asshole instead of a hero."

Kate remembered the photo of Jack Warner on the wall of Owen Sinclair's bedroom. "Did Mr. Sinclair name any individual in this building?"

She shook her head. "All of us moved in here way after it was over."

Mildred Coates, Kate remembered, had been here directly afterward. "Could he have named a relative of someone here?"

She gestured impatiently. "This is crap. If somebody was coming after Owen about HUAC, they'd have done it years ago."

Good point, Kate thought. She glanced at Taylor; he showed no indication of asking any further questions. She said, "You and Mr. Sinclair go back a long way, you told us. What did you mean by that?"

Maxine Marlowe picked up her drink and drained it. "One role I'd never play is a lady cop, and for good reason. Owen and me, we did exactly what you think, Miss Tight-Ass, and better than you can imagine. Give me that young body of yours, dearie, I wouldn't waste it being a tight-ass lady cop."

Washed by fury, Kate fought to not speak.

"My partner's been real tolerant." Taylor's voice seemed to Kate like a distant rumble. "But I've heard enough outta you. No police officer has to take —"

"I didn't kill Owen," Maxine Marlowe said to Taylor in sudden docility. "If I knocked off every no good cheating bastard in my life, they'd fill up a whole corner of Forest Lawn."

Kate had recovered her composure. "How long did you and Mr. Sinclair have a relationship?"

The actress shrugged. "Maybe six months, give or take a month. It ended more than ten years ago. Real ancient history."

"But you did feel some . . ." Kate chose the word deliberately, ". . . animosity."

Again the actress shrugged. "Sweetheart, you live and learn. And recover and forget. That's always been my motto."

Kate looked down at the circled name on her notepad. "You mentioned Paula being hurt."

"Well . . . not exactly Paula," said Maxine Marlowe. "It was Alice Goldstein, Paula's, ah . . . friend. Alice's dead, so it's ancient history too, just like everything else in the Beverly Malibu. Everything rolls off Paula, that snotty bitch. Finding Owen's body, you'd think she'd freak out like her niece did — but not her, she came out of that apartment just as cool as you please."

Kate chose not to pursue the topic of Paula Grant. She would hear about Paula's lover from

Paula herself and not, she thought poisonously, from this painted toad.

Taylor asked, "Do you know anyone who felt animosity toward the victim?"

Kate hid a smile at Taylor's choice of words.

The actress seemed not to notice. She was hesitating, looking away from Taylor. "Parker Thomas," she said. "Talk to Parker."

"What about?" Kate inquired with interest.

"Just talk to him."

"We intend to." Kate felt along the edge of the sofa for something substantive to help pull herself to her feet.

Maxine Marlowe got up and extended an assisting hand. "That sofa's a real son of a bitch," she said with a triumphant grin.

– 9 –

In the dimly lit first floor apartment, books were stacked everywhere — stuffed in corners, piled on chairs and tables. "They aren't all mine," Parker Thomas apologized, moving the contents of two rattan chairs to the floor. "A friend had to close her rare book store. I'm keeping some of the valuables here till she can work something out."

He wore a coarsely knit white pullover, baggy corduroys, battered jogging shoes. Through a full beard that seemed an extension of his bushy gray hair, his lips appeared thick and sensual. His eyes were pale sea green. A slight man, no more than five-two or -three, he had small hands and feet, and his shaggy head appeared too large for his body. Kate judged him to be in his early forties.

Seating herself in one of the rattan chairs, she asked, "How long have you lived here, Mr. Thomas?"

"Since 'seventy-two — sixteen years, right?" He perched on the arm of a small shabby sofa and picked up a pipe from an ashtray on top of some bound periodicals. His choice of seat, Kate noted, raised him to a height equal to hers and Taylor's. He continued, "I met Jerome Turner, we became good friends. I moved into the Beverly Malibu as soon as he had a vacancy."

Kate was examining the elaborately carved bowl of Thomas's pipe. The apartment smelled pleasurably of its smoke. She smiled. "A meerschaum?"

He nodded and grinned, revealing large and very white teeth.

"A beauty," she said.

"My greatest treasure. Eighteen years in the breaking in."

"I can tell. My father used one for nearly thirty years." That meerschaum pipe had been so much a part of her father that she had buried it with him. She asked, "How well did you know Mr. Sinclair?"

"Very well. About as well as anyone." He said easily, "You know of course that he was a HUAC stool pigeon."

She nodded. Obviously Parker Thomas would not be reticent with information.

"Jerome actually wanted to have him in this building, he was fascinated with him. The way he studied Sinclair, you'd think he was trying to

104

decipher the Mona Lisa." Parker Thomas was smiling broadly. "Jerome Turner, you see, believed in the divinity of man. He was positive that one day Sinclair would wake up to find out he had a conscience, he'd become Raskolnikov in *Crime and Punishment.* Jerome couldn't believe Sinclair was as banal in his evil as he actually was. Jerome kept poking at him, waiting for the day he'd crack open and show a gleam of divinity." Parker Thomas was chuckling.

Kate was smiling in spite of herself. "I take it you didn't share Turner's belief."

"In no way. I'm a trained historian."

Taylor entered the conversation: "Meaning what?" His tone was confrontational. Kate remembered that among Taylor's prejudices were small men, and men with beards or otherwise unconventional hair.

"Meaning what," Parker Thomas repeated thoughtfully. Looking at Taylor, he stroked his beard lightly and puffed from his pipe; the sweet rich scent of maple reached Kate. "Not much, now that you question it. Jerome after all was correct in believing that the hearings were America's version of the Inquisition."

"I was a young man in those days," Taylor said, stretching out in his chair and propping a foot against a stack of leatherbound Faulkner. Kate saw Thomas's fleeting wince. "Funny, I don't remember a single soul being burned at the stake."

Kate smothered a sigh. Taylor was a fool to challenge this man in the stronghold of his expertise.

"No, we didn't go that far," Thomas said. "But like the three Christian Inquisitions, our heretics lost their civil rights, were exiled, had their property confiscated."

"That's crazy," Taylor stated. "None of that happened."

"No?" Thomas leaned forward and pushed up the sleeves of his pullover as if in relish of combat. "A blacklist prevented our heretics from working at their chosen professions. We put heretics like the Hollywood Ten in jail for their political beliefs. We persecuted our other heretics with so much hate they had to move from the communities they'd lived and worked in all their lives."

"This was different," Taylor argued. "In the fifties Communism was spreading everywhere."

"Exactly what the Inquisitors said about heresy in the Christian world. And back then, anyone who wasn't a heretic but ever associated with heretics was ordered to repent under pain of excommunication by identifying them. Doesn't all that put you in mind of a certain Wisconsin senator?"

"Communism is *real*," Taylor growled. He gestured at Kate. "My partner and me, we got free trips to Vietnam and Korea to prove it."

"I fought in Vietnam, too," Parker Thomas said. "But in our own country, was Communism ever the threat McCarthy claimed it was? He never proved it, he never proved anything he claimed. He came to this town and destroyed lives — and never came up with one shred of proof that Communist dogma ever infiltrated our movies. Or anything else, for that matter."

"Gentlemen," Kate said, "perhaps you could continue this interesting discussion later." Entertained, reluctant to interrupt, she knew she must rescue Taylor. She asked Parker Thomas, "When did you come to the party yesterday?"

Drawing on his pipe, he focused his pale green eyes on her. "Shortly before one. Mildred Coates and I were there first, we helped Hazel put her platters of food around."

"Did you notice when Mr. Sinclair arrived?"

"Maxine Marlowe came sashaying in with Sinclair right behind her. I didn't notice when. I do remember he had a bottle of bourbon under his arm."

"We understand you argued with him."

He made an off-hand gesture. "Just the usual. Dorothy Brennan asked some questions, Cyril Crane and I got into it again with Sinclair and Dudley Kincaid."

"I take it you don't agree with Dudley Kincaid either," she commented.

"It's so hard to disagree with Dudley." His tone was sarcastic. "Dudley never fought in any war. But he regrets having only one life to give to demanding that others give their lives for his country."

Amused, but unwilling to be sidetracked, Kate said, "So there was a great deal of hostility between you and Mr. Sinclair."

"I'd rank myself a distant number two in that regard."

"Oh? Who's number one?"

"Dudley Kincaid."

Surprised, Kate studied his pale green eyes. They were unreadable. "Why?"

"I happen to know that Dudley Kincaid wrote a screenplay Owen Sinclair stole."

"How do you know?" Taylor was sitting up, looking at Thomas with interest. "Sinclair tell you this?"

"Of course not."

"So where do you get your info?"

Again Thomas stroked his beard. He looked at Kate. "I'm a historical researcher, I supply background and fact verification for film and television scripts. I did some fact-checking on a nineteen seventy-four film called *Confederate Night.* Do you happen to know of it?"

Kate and Taylor shook their heads.

Thomas shook his own head ruefully. "*Confederate Night* followed a war strategist attached to Jefferson Davis's inner circle. It was original work, a fine film, technically brilliant, much admired by people who really know our business. But it got limited distribution. Sinclair sold the idea to Jeremiah Ashton, a good old southern boy whose name is on the film as screen writer. But the basic script was Dudley's. He knew it, Ashton knew it, Sinclair knew it, I knew it."

Taylor was busy writing. "You have any proof of this?"

"No. And neither does Dudley. Sinclair and Jeremiah Ashton weren't about to admit where Ashton got all that detail for his screenplay. They claimed pure coincidence."

"So why didn't Dudley Kincaid sue?" Taylor asked. "You hear all the time about that kind of lawsuit."

"He couldn't prove his claim. With the paucity of original ideas in this town, any professional screen writer including Dudley knows to register his work with the Screen Writers' Guild. But he hadn't done it, he was still polishing the script. He let Sinclair see it, and Sinclair stole it."

"So essentially this is unprovable conjecture," Kate said in disappointment.

Parker shrugged. "From your point of view, so what? Dudley knows Sinclair stole his work. And Dudley hasn't written a line since nineteen seventy-four, he's had writer's block ever since. What I'm saying is, he felt one hell of a lot more hostile toward Sinclair than I ever could."

"The party yesterday," Kate said. "How much time would you say you spent arguing with Mr. Sinclair?"

"Off and on for the whole time, really." Thomas's strong white teeth flashed in the briefest of smiles. "A very long time, it seemed to me."

"Did you notice anything Mr. Sinclair ate or drank?"

"This is an important question, isn't it." Thomas put down his pipe, briefly stroked his beard, then picked up a book from beside him and riffled its pages. He finally answered, "We were standing at the far end of the table, away from the television set. Sinclair's bourbon bottle was there, he was drinking from a dixie cup, he kept refilling it —"

"Where was the bourbon bottle?" Taylor interrupted. "How far away from him?"

"At his elbow. Right on the table beside him."

"Did he move around much?"

"No. He was right beside the platters of pastrami and potato salad he was helping himself from."

Kate asked, "Between the times that he drank from the dixie cup, did he hold onto the cup or leave it on the table?"

"He left it on the table," Thomas said

immediately. "Sinclair couldn't talk without using his hands, he had to put the cup down."

Kate paused to record this answer, chiding herself that she had not previously widened her questions to Cyril Crane, one of those who had argued with Sinclair, to include these more precise details. She would have to verify these statements of Thomas's with him and with the other tenants present at the party.

"What did the rest of you drink?"

"Hazel's punch." He smiled. "It was really pretty good. Although Dudley spiked his with some of Sinclair's bourbon."

Kate looked at him sharply. "Did anyone else?"

Again he riffled the pages of the book for a while. "Not that I recall."

"What did he eat besides pastrami and potato salad?"

"Corned beef, and lots of it. But the rest of us didn't exactly stint, either. It was from Nate 'n Al's, after all."

"And so you ate while you were arguing?"

"Sure. The food was right there where we were standing, everybody else was milling around the table, too. It was a real nice spread."

"We understand there was a point where Mr. Sinclair complained of not feeling well. Do you remember that?"

He nodded. "I assumed it was more of his stomach trouble. He'd been complaining for months. At least that's what we all thought it was. Until . . ." He shrugged.

"Do you know if Mr. Sinclair ever consulted a doctor about his complaint?"

"I'm pretty sure he didn't. Even after he started losing weight I remember him saying a doctor would just tell him to stop drinking, and he could do that himself when he was ready."

"Thank you, Mr. Thomas," Kate said, closing her notebook. "We'll probably have other questions."

Parker Thomas fixed his strange eyes on her. "From the way Paula was so frozen about what she'd seen, I gather Sinclair's demise was a nasty business."

"We don't recommend it," Taylor said.

"Dying the way he did," Thomas said, "losing his son in Vietnam — none of it begins to make up for the lives he laid waste to."

Taylor said in clear annoyance, "You think Sinclair being an informer makes him real scum, right?"

"Scum." Parker cocked his head to one side, mulling over the word. "Not too bad a term. I'd say it fits him."

Taylor said, "Doesn't your telling us about Dudley Kincaid make you an informer too?"

Again Thomas pushed up his sleeves. "The House Committee on Un-American Activities had no constitutional license whatever to hunt down and destroy American citizens. The informers who turned over their fellow citizens for persecution had no moral justification to do it either. Murder, however, is a crime."

Thomas sighed, closed the book he had been

holding, and placed it back on the stack. Kate saw that the book was *The Making of the President, 1960* by Theodore H. White. "Sometimes," Parker Thomas muttered, "sometimes I think all the best people are dead."

Thinking of her father and mother, and of Anne, Kate answered silently: Sometimes so do I.

– 10 –

Kate and Taylor were in the community room with the door closed, having adjourned their interviews to compare impressions.

"I got two possibles," Taylor announced. "The jealous bag of wrinkles across the hall, and Dudley Kincaid. If the info pans out from the bearded shrimp downstairs."

Kate inferred that he meant Maxine Marlowe and Parker Thomas. Curious, she asked, "Why do you say Maxine is jealous?"

"You're kidding, right? I bet my paycheck she's a bitch around any woman younger than her."

Ruefully remembering her entrapment in Maxine Marlowe's devouring sofa, Kate was gratified that Taylor had placed the most generous interpretation possible on her encounter with the actress.

He added, "I did like her perfume, though."

"Did you," she managed to say.

"Maxine, she's a good possible, she's the woman spurned," he argued. "Go ahead, say I'm a male chauvinist — but this killing fits a woman." He waved toward Owen Sinclair's apartment. "This poison-torture stuff is something a woman would dream up."

"Right," she responded, leafing back through her notes of their interviews, "you're a chauvinist."

When he did not respond she looked over at him. He was slumped in the chair across the table from her, sitting sideways, a foot up on an adjacent chair. She was aware of her own energy level ebbing. They needed this break.

She kicked her shoes off and put her own feet up on the chair next to her. "The cruelty of this killing tells me it was revenge, Ed. From what Parker Thomas told us, Kincaid could be our best possible. Maybe the victim did steal his script. Maybe Kincaid became more and more bitter about not being able to write anything since. What do you say?"

"Damn good motive," Taylor admitted.

"What do you think about the argument at the party, the politics business?"

"I think it's got nothing to do with nothing."

114

She was surprised. "Why?"

"For chrissakes Kate. It was thirty-five years ago."

There was a knock on the door. A voice called, "Hello, it's me, Hazel!"

"Jesus," grumbled Taylor, pulling himself to his feet to open the door.

Hazel marched in carrying a pot of coffee and two mugs on a tray. "I know you two can use this," she declared. She set the tray down on the table. "I know Mildred offered you coffee, but Maxine and Parker have the manners of a baboon."

The detectives chimed their thanks. Taylor said, "How did you know we were in here? And where we've been?"

She patted the urn in the pocket of her housecoat. "Jerome and me, we know what goes on in our Beverly Malibu." She marched out the door, slamming it behind her.

"To Hazel," Taylor said, raising his coffee mug. "May she not be our killer."

"Indeed," Kate said, clinking her mug with his and taking a deep and satisfying swallow of the fresh hot brew. "About the argument at the party, Ed. Let's look at it. We've got Cyril Crane and Mildred Coates personally affected by the subject of that argument, the blacklist. From what Maxine said, Paula Grant is another. We need to talk to her about that." A prospect, Kate acknowledged, that she welcomed.

Taylor shrugged. "Yeah, well, so what? I know we need to check out who Sinclair named, but I'm betting it's nobody here — and nobody connected with anybody here. Like Maxine said, why wait all this time to knock Sinclair off?"

"Maybe it's been festering, like Dudley Kincaid and his writer's block."

"I don't buy it. I don't even buy this writer's block shit. Somebody does something bad enough to make you kill them, you don't sit around for years before you do it."

She shrugged concession. "Okay, let's look at the crime scenario. We've got ten people at the party not counting the victim. For now I say we cross out Aimee Grant and Houston — no motive."

"You still figuring somebody came in there and watched him croak?"

Grimly visualizing the red kitchen chair beside the bed, she nodded.

Taylor said, "We know for sure somebody came in there and cuffed him. But I still say the killer maybe split right after. I still say the red chair maybe doesn't mean what we think it does."

But it does, Kate thought.

"Because if Crane's with Houston and Paula's with Aimee, then it rules all of 'em out, unless we got people in cahoots. You ready to rule out Crane or Paula Grant stepping out of their apartments for a quick minute, to cuff him and leave?"

"No," she said. In a homicide committed with this much boldness, she could not rule out one more bold act.

She tore a page from her notebook and laid it on the table. "Okay. So we've got eight suspects." She sketched a rectangle representing the community room, looking around her as she drew. "There's the

TV where Aimee and Houston were. And here's where Crane, Thomas, Kincaid, and Dorothy Brennan were standing with the victim beside the table. So that leaves Maxine, Paula, Hazel, and Mildred Coates."

"Mildred Coates," Taylor said. He looked uncomfortable. "I say we cross her out."

She decided not to tease him. "She does have a motive, Ed," she pointed out. "What happened to her husband and her own career — maybe it took thirty-five years to fester into the murder of a stand-in for her husband's informer."

"I can't buy it. That tottery old lady hooking Sinclair up with cuffs? No way."

She shook her head at him. He could be so contradictory — on the one hand believing that a woman most likely committed this pitiless crime, yet underestimating the true capacity of women to act. "I can't agree with you, Ed. Let's say we have seven-and-a-half suspects."

"This Dorothy Brennan, being here not even a year . . ."

She stared at him. "You want to take a suspect off the list before we even talk to her, check her out?"

He sat up in his chair. "Did I say that? So we got eight suspects, four of 'em around Sinclair and four milling around the room."

"From what Hazel told us, it appears our killer stole a key to this apartment during the Fourth of July party. We know Dudley Kincaid was drinking from Sinclair's bottle. So the killer didn't put the strychnine in the bottle before Sinclair brought it with him — the lab should verify that when it tests the bottles and party debris. But why poison the victim at the party? Why take such a risk when the killer had access to his apartment to poison him any time?"

"That's easy, Kate. Nobody took Sinclair's keys. He really did lose them." Taylor was making a list in his notebook.

"Maybe," she said grudgingly. "But it seems just too coincidental."

"So right now we need to interview Kincaid and Dorothy Brennan," Taylor said. "That'll cover everybody at the party. Then we get the record of Sinclair's testimony and see who he did name, cover that base." From the eagerness in his voice, Kate could tell that Hazel's coffee had restored his energy. "We're gonna crack this one, Kate. We're close, I can feel it."

Her own spirits had picked up. "We have to be careful, Ed. Our information about Dudley Kincaid isn't provable. So we don't want to confront him with it. We need him to volunteer, to talk about Sinclair's theft himself."

"I say we talk to Dorothy Brennan first," Taylor said. "Leave Kincaid for last. You talk to Paula, clean up that loose end. I'll get with the FBI about getting into Sinclair's file. Then we take somebody in for heavy duty interrogation."

Kate smiled. "You really want me to interview Paula by myself? Forego a chance to gaze at the gorgeous Aimee?"

His expression was doleful. "I dunno, Kate, I get funny vibrations inside that apartment of Paula's." Then he grinned at her. "I figured out who Aimee looks like. Candice Bergen. I'm crazy about Candice Bergen."

Aren't we all, she thought. "Ed," she said, "Candice Bergen is blonde. With brown eyes. Aimee's brunette. With . . ." She groped to describe the blue-violet of Aimee Grant's eyes.

"Eyes the color of Liz Taylor's," he finished for her. "I still say she looks like Candice Bergen."

– 11 –

Dorothy Brennan led Kate and Taylor into her apartment, her tall, ample figure moving slowly, a mid-length skirt revealing big solid calves and large feet laced into low-heeled shoes. Her body was decidedly triangular: narrow-shouldered, small-chested, with heavy hips and legs and feet seeming to bind her into the firmament.

She waved the detectives to an obviously new, comfortable-looking sofa, then dropped her body into a flimsy Danish-modern armchair which made faint cracking sounds as it received her. Her dark brown eyes fastening on Kate with lively curiosity, she pulled a crocheted shawl around her, then tucked a strand of hair back into the unruly mass from which it had escaped. The thick gray hair was so carelessly simple in style that Kate suspected it had been home cut.

She glanced at Dorothy Brennan's left hand. It bore a wide gold wedding band. Another widow, she surmised. Actuarial statistics dictated the probability of widowhood to most of the women in the Beverly Malibu, but this woman appeared to be only in her early sixties. The building seemed to have more than its share of solitary women.

Through the glass doors leading to a long, narrow, high-walled patio Kate saw a soothing green forest of plants. Unbuttoning her jacket, sitting back on the sofa, she felt at ease amid the homey, cluttered comfort of this small apartment. The coffee table in front of her with issues of *The National Review* and sections of the *Los Angeles Times* strewn across it; a gray formica desk near the patio door with a jumble of books, their plastic-swathed dust jackets indicating library origin; the framed family photos in disarray on a table, as if they were picked up and looked at so often that organization was not even a consideration.

"Mrs. Brennan," Kate began, "we're here to ask you to help us reconstruct some of the events of yesterday."

"Please do call me Dorothy." The full smile, readily given, deepened all the crows' feet around her eyes. And was somewhat inappropriate, Kate thought, given the grim circumstances of their presence here. But so far no one in the Beverly Malibu, except for

Hazel Turner, had seemed in any way distressed by the death of Owen Sinclair.

Dorothy continued, "All I can tell you is, yesterday I joined the festivities shortly after one-thirty, and anyone who hadn't gone off for the day was already there, including Mr. Sinclair." The slightly husky voice was energetic, expressive.

"We understand there was some kind of an argument," Taylor said. "Could you tell us about that?" His tone was courteous; but Kate knew that he saw no need for indulging in preliminary small talk to establish rapport with this witness.

"Surely," answered Dorothy. "There indeed was an argument — started by me, I'm afraid. It grew quite heated. Especially on the part of Mr. Kincaid."

Unwilling to accept Taylor's lead into specifics quite this soon, Kate asked, smiling, "Do I hear some sort of accent or inflection in your voice?"

Again there was the wide, easy smile. "Other people have mentioned it. Perhaps I'm a natural mimic. My husband's family is English, I must have picked something up from his mother." She gestured to the table of photos. "I lived with Elisabeth these last fourteen years after my husband's death. She passed on early this year, she —"

"Who was arguing with who?" Taylor interrupted.

Kate looked at him in annoyance.

Dorothy flicked a glance over him, her face becoming impassive. She said to Kate, "Mostly it was Mr. Kincaid arguing with Mr. Thomas, who was the soul of calm. I realize I instigated the whole thing, but I had no idea that I would. Well, of course I knew Mr. Sinclair was an informer —"

"How did you know?" Kate inquired.

Her brow furrowing, Dorothy restored another escaping strand of hair. "Why, it's common knowledge here in the Beverly Malibu, and I do talk to the other tenants, of course. They're quite friendly to me."

They would be, Kate thought. There was warmth and receptiveness in this woman, a motherly quality that invited confidences. "Please go on."

Dorothy gestured to a small portable TV on a metal stand. "I saw a program over the weekend about the blacklist and the Hollywood Ten. With a real live informer right here in this building, I couldn't resist asking Mr. Sinclair what he thought about a statement of Dalton Trumbo's about the blacklist years. And that started it all."

"What did Dalton Trumbo say?" Kate asked, turning to a fresh page in her notebook.

"That there were no villains or heroes or saints or devils, there were only victims."

Dorothy pulled herself to her feet and went over to the patio, slid back the door. Cool air inundated the room. As Kate wrote down this argument–precipitating statement, she could hear the hiss of distant traffic, the caroling of birds. A thought struck her: this was the only apartment so far whose occupant apparently did not smoke. She turned to another fresh page and scrawled a reminder to check the lab findings for brands of cigarette butts in the trash in Owen Sinclair's apartment.

"Would you perhaps like a soft drink?" Dorothy asked. "Some iced tea?"

"Thank you, we've just had coffee," Kate replied.

Dorothy returned to her chair, which again protested as it received her bulk. "So I asked Mr. Sinclair what he thought about that statement. But it was Mr. Thomas who answered. He said it was generous of Dalton Trumbo to forgive his own victimizers, but he couldn't speak for anyone else — and informers could never ever be equated morally with their victims."

Dorothy raised her hands and heaved a sigh. "Well, Mr. Kincaid really jumped into it then, shouting something about cooperative witnesses being the ones who'd suffered most, when all they'd been was patriotic. It turned into a real free-for-all, and here I'd started it. I can't tell you how I felt — all I'd wanted was an answer to the one question. I hope you won't make me try to remember every part of that whole argument."

"Not right now," Taylor said.

Irritated at his impatience with this interview, Kate asked, "Did they argue about the blacklist the entire time?"

"Oh no, they got off onto all sorts of other tangents. Iran, Grenada, South Africa — and Vietnam. Everybody really got into it over Vietnam including me, I must confess. Mr. Sinclair lost a son over there, you know."

"Yes," Kate said.

"Well, you can lose children on many sorts of battlefields. I lost my own son several years ago to drugs, and that's a battlefield with carnage beyond description. I know you people do what you can, and it must be terrible to have to go in there and pick up all the broken bodies. But I suspect you have no idea what it's like to be helpless on the sidelines. To watch your own child disintegrate, and not be able to do a thing . . ."

"It is terrible," Kate said softly. "I'm sorry, Dorothy."

"I've got two boys of my own," Taylor said, closing his notebook and looking sympathetically at Dorothy. "They're grown, but I still worry about one of 'em getting hooked."

Dorothy nodded. "Indeed you should."

Kate asked, to change the subject as much as to gain other information, "How long have you lived here?"

"Since March. Nine months now."

Another cool breeze wafted in the patio door. Kate breathed it in. A siren wailed in the distance. "The patio door," she said, a thought occurring. "Did you have it open yesterday any time after the party?"

"Why . . . yes. I often do, unless the weather is quite cool."

Kate leaned forward eagerly. This apartment was on the same side of the building as Owen Sinclair's, one over from Mildred Coates. "Did you hear anything? Anything out of the ordinary?"

"I heard Mr. Sinclair's music, I always did whenever I worked on my plants or had my door open. Why . . . now that you mention it, there was something a bit odd. It was opera music."

"Opera?" Taylor repeated. He flipped open his notebook.

"Opera, and I can't say I was happy about it. All these months I'd never heard him play opera. I didn't mind his other music, he kept his windows closed usually so it didn't bother me the way it did Paula and Maxine and Mildred. But opera . . ." She turned her palms up as if in apology. "Sorry, it sounds like screeching to me."

"Me too," Taylor said, busy writing.

"I had to close my door. And every time I opened it, that screeching was still going on. He must have had quite a stack of records playing."

Kate did not look at Taylor. "When did the music start, and how long would you say it lasted?"

"Well, it started right after the party ended, which was around three." She reflected. "Let's see, I put some water on for tea around a quarter to six, and opened the door again. It had stopped by then."

Kate gazed sightlessly at the photos on the table across from her. Paula Grant had discovered the body at five minutes to six. So Owen Sinclair's death cries, disguised by opera music, had lasted more than two and a half hours . . .

Kate's gaze sharpened on the photos, individual and group shots of children up to the teen years. "I take it these are your children?"

"Yes. Two daughters and a son."

"Dorothy, why did you spend Thanksgiving here yesterday, and not with one of your children?"

Dorothy shook her head, ran both hands through her hair. "I suppose you have to ask these questions, don't you." The warmth had vanished from her face, the energy from her voice. She pointed to the photos. "You know about my son. Colleen, my youngest, is living in England and hasn't seen fit to come home in fifteen years. My other child took herself from us when she was eleven years old, with my husband's pistol."

Unable to immediately speak, Kate thought numbly, So much death in this woman's life. Just as in her own life . . .

"Ma'am, my condolences," Taylor offered in subdued tones.

"You've had a great deal of tragedy," Kate murmured.

Dorothy smiled faintly. "They say it toughens you. I haven't noticed."

"Did you know Mr. Sinclair before you moved into this building?"

"Know him?" She looked perplexed. "I never saw him before in my life."

"What do you do for a living?"

"I'm sixty-three, the age of uselessness. I'm retired." Her tone was growing increasingly testy.

"You're still quite young, ma'am," Taylor said. "And you look young."

"Thank you. But sixty-three isn't young in the workaday world."

This apartment had to cost a minimum of six hundred a month in this area, Kate estimated, and probably more. Its modest furnishings indicated that Dorothy Brennan was not blessed with funds. "What *did* you do for a living?"

"I worked as a secretary. For a number of firms. After my husband passed on." The dark eyes had become cold, distant.

"We have to ask these questions, Dorothy," Kate said.

"I realize that. But I don't relish being pried at any more than anyone would." She continued somberly, "When my husband's mother died last year, she left enough money that I could move into a decent apartment in a decent area."

"It's a nice part of town," Taylor commented, again closing his notebook.

"Safe," Dorothy said. "Safer than many areas of the city."

Her face filling with realization, she shook her head and said ruefully, "How very ludicrous to say that, after what's happened. I was thinking of drugs, and gangs."

"Of course," Kate said. "Tell us, did Mr. Sinclair ever answer the question about Dalton Trumbo that started the argument?"

"Yes. I can tell you his answer exactly: 'Honey, never look back, what's done is done — that's my motto. I never lost one second of sleep over anything I did.' "

Getting to her feet, buttoning her jacket, Kate asked, "What did you think about that answer?"

"Why . . . knowing him and what he did, it didn't surprise me at all."

But to Kate, Dorothy Brennan had seemed oddly surprised by the question.

— 12 —

Dudley Kincaid's rounded, bony shoulders were hunched inside a gray western shirt adorned by a bolo tie fastened with a piece of turquoise. His baggy brown trousers were held up by suspenders. Over a small pinched mouth a coarse gray moustache was shaved above the lip line and trimmed off blunt at the ends. A few dozen long strands of yellowish hair were combed back over his pate. As he smiled in welcome, his blue eyes, framed by steel-rimmed trifocals, seemed to partially submerge in the surrounding crinkles and folds of loose flesh.

The dim, tidy living room was furnished with a sofa, an armchair, and a recliner, all of them of shabby walnut-brown leather. From the room's stale cigarette smoke Kate separated out an additional odor evoking memory of dutiful childhood visits to her grandmother in a Grand Blanc, Michigan rest home, and the faintly sour smell of ailing, fragile old people shut away from fresh air and sunshine.

Kincaid eased himself into the recliner and cranked a handle on the side to pop out the bottom section which elevated his feet. Taylor settled himself on the sofa, and Kate sat in the armchair, its fissured leather whooshing under her weight. Several blue-backed manuscripts lay on the coffee table before her; more were stacked on a cluttered desk near the window, a goose-neck lamp providing additional strong light. Obviously Kincaid had been working before she and Taylor had entered.

Kate began with her standard question: "How long have you lived here, sir?"

"Twenty-one years." The voice was an authoritative rumble.

"And how long have you known Mr. Sinclair?"

A thumb and forefinger caressing his moustache, he considered her question. "I believe I was twenty. That would make it since nineteen thirty-nine."

So Dudley Kincaid was sixty-nine years old. The bent posture of his bony frame suggested he was ten years older. Of the older people in this building, Kate reflected, Mildred Coates had been defeated by her life, but Hazel Turner had refused to concede even her husband's death, much less her own mortality; and Maxine Marlowe, clown-like though she might appear, had refused to be worn down by the passage of the years. And Paula Grant . . . Kate smiled to herself.

"How did the two of you end up in the same building?" Taylor inquired in his most affable tone. Obviously he meant to ingratiate himself with their most promising suspect.

Kincaid peered at Taylor through the top part of his trifocals. "Owen talked me into moving here after Genevieve — my wife — died. That was in 'sixty-seven. I've been here ever since."

Taylor followed up. "So you were on good terms with him?"

With nicotine-stained fingers Kincaid shook an unfiltered Camel from a crumpled pack. He opened a small box of wooden matches, scraped a match four times along the abrasive strip before the match flared. "Sure," he answered Taylor's question, and lit his cigarette.

What a lot of stupid business to go through to smoke, Kate thought in irritation. She asked, "Were you friends?"

"Friendship is a subjective term," Kincaid replied. But he was tapping his cigarette with metronome-like precision on his ashtray, and his narrowing eyes seemed almost to disappear amid pleats of flesh as he stared at her.

"Did you spend time with him socially?"

Kincaid said slowly, "We observed all the customary amenities among those occupying the same building."

"So you were civil."

"Correct."

Kate studied Dudley Kincaid. The man seemed not the least skilled at subterfuge. "You knew each other from the time you were young men. Owen Sinclair wanted you to move into this building. Obviously your relationship with him cooled. Why?"

The ember of Dudley Kincaid's cigarette glowed as he pulled smoke deep into his lungs. Kate felt her own lungs tighten in rejection. It had been seventeen years since she smoked, and she had smoked more than a pack a day back then, but never unfiltered cigarettes.

"Grievances accumulate over the years," Dudley Kincaid rumbled. "They've got nothing whatever to do with this, with his death."

She pointed with her pen to the stack of manuscripts. "We understand you're a screen writer." She would approach him more obliquely about what Parker Thomas had revealed.

"Those aren't mine." He leaned his head back against the recliner. "I'm blocked, you see."

She nodded sympathetically.

He drew in more smoke and expelled a huge grey cloud as he sighed. "These days I repair scripts. Agents at William Morris funnel them to me." His smile was self-deprecating. "Even though I can't seem to use my talent for my own benefit, I still do have it. My writer's block is probably just as well."

He jabbed a knobby finger at the stack of scripts, his smile mutating into a scowl. "Trash. Utter garbage. I never see a script with a scintilla of originality. Screen writing today is a joke. This town doesn't produce two decent movies a year. And the cretins running TV networks — they consider experience a detriment. If you're over thirty you might as well be dead, you have nothing left to say."

Taylor said, "We hear there was some bad feeling between the victim and the women in this building."

Kincaid seemed as disconcerted as Kate at this change in focus. Taylor's tone had cooled; Kate suspected that he resented Kincaid's contempt for the industry that provided his own movie-watching pleasures.

"Well . . . yes, the women had their complaints about him." Kincaid waved a dismissive hand. "Minor business, really. Although I suppose Maxine's entitled to a hard feeling or two."

Kate chose her words. "We understand she had some animosity toward Mr. Sinclair."

"Poor Maxine. Femme fatale, sexual paragon — superior to all other members of her sex. Then Owen got hold of her." His sarcasm became condescension. "Owen wasn't a bit discriminating when it came to women. Any skirt that came along caught his attention — until he got what was under it. The only reason he married so often was the morality of the times. Those women insisted on a marriage license before their skirts came off. Owen was always, very simply, a goat. A goat who became an old goat." He chuckled, obviously pleased with this last phrase.

Taylor said, "So she's carried a grudge."

"Don't quote me on that," Kincaid protested, holding up a hand. "If you're insinuating she killed him, I'd think she'd have done it long ago when he milked her for all he could then kicked her in the teeth. Like he did everybody else who was ever good to him."

Kate said quickly, "Like you, Mr. Kincaid?"

He took another deep drag on his cigarette; it had

burned down almost to his yellow fingers. Peering at her over the top of his glasses, he said, "I was thinking of his wives and children. And Maxine. Although she's ignored his existence for the better part of the last decade. And he was more than annoyed by that, I can tell you. So if she was still smarting over him, she's had some measure of satisfaction. At this point I have no idea who'd kill Owen, or why. He was no more deceitful to her than he was to . . . to anyone else in his life."

Kate said, "Like you, Mr. Kincaid?"

"Exactly what are you driving at?" he demanded.

She deflected him: "Did you ever work for Mr. Sinclair?"

Kincaid took one final drag from his Camel and extinguished it. Kate looked at the remaining half an inch of cigarette butt. With such lethal smoking habits, how could this man have survived sixty-nine years?

"We collaborated on screenplays in the old days," Kincaid said. "Ideas of mine he converted into pap. He cheapened and dirtied every creative thing he touched, he was incapable of doing otherwise."

"That happened only in the old days?" Kate asked with careful emphasis. "*Only* in the old days?"

"The old days were the only good days Owen ever had. He had no talent whatsoever." The blue eyes became glacial behind the glasses, but Kincaid spoke softly. "Owen craved respect. He dreamed of being a John Ford, a Billy Wilder. To direct or write just one quality film. He even dreamed of becoming another Noel Coward." His eyes glinted with mockery. "You should have seen his drivel, his pitiful, witless attempts at writing movies and plays. What a legacy," he said with a satisfaction that was no less savage for his quiet tone. "A failed movie maker whose films are disintegrating in UCLA's film archives. A failed screen writer and playwright. A failed husband and father."

Kate digested this, noting that Kincaid had not mentioned what might be Sinclair's one claim to history, if not fame. "Mr. Sinclair was not a popular person with much of anyone in the Beverly Malibu," she observed. "Why don't you tell us what he did to lose your friendship?"

"I've answered that question before," he said testily. He ran a hand over the sparse hairs on his head. "It simply took me longer than it should have to realize he wasn't terribly representative as a human being."

Taylor came at him from another direction. "We understand there was an argument of some kind at the party."

He shrugged. "Dorothy Brennan brought up the business about the blacklist. And of course Parker Thomas and Cyril Crane got into it again with Owen and me."

"What did you get into? Explain that to us."

"Parker Thomas claims he's not a Communist." Kincaid's voice had strengthened. "Well, maybe he's not, but let me tell you he's the biggest Commie-lover between here and Moscow. What Owen Sinclair did for America and HUAC was his duty. But Commie-lovers like Parker Thomas and fellow travelers like Cyril Crane try to talk everybody into thinking Owen's some sort of pariah. Parker Thomas and his ilk would just -as soon see the hammer and sickle fly over our country as ever defend it against its enemies."

Kate made a pretense of checking through her notebook. "Our information says Mr. Thomas did indeed fight for this country."

"He got *drafted*."

Kate said innocently, "We assume you volunteered?"

"Inner ear dysfunction," Kincaid grated, his face wrathful. "I was four-F."

"So," Kate said, "even though you withdrew your friendship from Mr. Sinclair, you approved of his testimony before the House Committee enough to defend him to Mr. Thomas and Mr. Crane — correct?"

Kincaid shook out another Camel and began his match-scraping ceremony again. "His testimony and my . . . distaste for him are unrelated." He said judiciously, "Anyone who really understands what this country is all about understands that Owen did the right thing. His testimony was his patriotic duty. And he paid a price for it like many patriotic Americans have — from Patrick Henry to Oliver North."

She studied him. Such certainty, such purity of belief must be comforting. And a man who permitted no gray areas in his beliefs was a man of simple solutions . . .

She said, "The Committee was disbanded some time ago, was it not?"

"In 'seventy-five. Look what's happened since. Communist dogma infiltrating both political parties, our classrooms, our movies, our books," he ticked off on his fingers. "The fruits of labor from decent, hard-working Americans redistributed to people who don't deserve them. This Gorbachev– *glasnost* business — even Ronald Reagan's been duped. We're rotting from within just like Khrushchev —"

Taylor said, "You know anything about the people whose names he gave to the Committee?"

"I don't even remember their names now," Kincaid answered. "That was years ago. As I said yesterday, as you sow, so shall you reap. Anything bad that happened to any of them, they deserved it."

"Mr. Kincaid," Kate said with deliberate slowness, "do you have anything to add, anything at all, to what you've told us about your relationship with Mr. Sinclair?"

Pulling deeply on his cigarette, he stared coldly at her. "I've answered every one of your questions. I've been completely cooperative."

She had heard enough. There were many more questions for Dudley Kincaid, and in her judgment she and Taylor should gather additional information so that the questions could be asked in the setting of a formal interrogation. They needed to quickly finish their preliminary investigation.

She nodded to Taylor, who tapped his notebook, his signal of understanding and agreement.

"Mr. Kincaid," Kate said, "my partner and I have other questions but we'll need to ask them a bit later. Would you excuse us?"

He looked at her in sudden uncertainty. "Of course," he said.

– 13 –

Aimee Grant answered the door to Paula Grant's apartment.

Taylor's knees would buckle, Kate thought as she surveyed the loosely knit maroon sweater that outlined high and shapely breasts, the stone-washed jeans that clasped the young woman's legs all the way down to the ankles.

"Detective Delafield, please come in," Paula Grant called in her Lauren Bacall tones. She reclined in a corner of the sofa, sitting sideways, her dark pants and gray sweater blending with the black and white tweed fabric, one leg stretched out and the other drawn up, an arm draped over the knee, smoke curling up from the cigarette she held.

Graceful, Kate thought. The woman is so graceful.

As she had earlier that morning, Paula Grant cast an impassive glance over Kate's jacket and pants. But she smiled — a guarded smile — and Kate was annoyed at the gratitude she felt; she needed to master her sense of inferiority to this woman.

Kate chose the same sling chair she had occupied the night before. Aimee sat beside her. On the muted television screen football players flung their brightly armored bodies together, accompanied by low volume music emanating from two small speakers that flanked the windows; Kate recognized the falsetto notes of the Bee Gees. On the coffee table in front of Aimee were an untouched toasted cheese sandwich and a can of diet Coke, and a paperback turned face-down.

Aimee Grant had taken over this apartment, Kate thought with an emotion close to resentment. Her football game, her music, her food, her book.

"May we get you a sandwich," Paula offered. "I've just finished lunch, but you can keep Aimee company."

"Thank you, no," Kate said. She would eat later, when Taylor returned.

"Share my sandwich," Aimee said, "I'm not hungry."

"Neither am I," Kate said, realizing the fact with surprise.

"Aimee, do try to eat," Paula said. "You need

to." She said to Kate, "Perhaps something to drink, then?" She indicated the goblet on the table beside her. "Would you join me in a glass of wine?"

In dry-mouthed reaction to the note of warmth and intimacy in the low, husky tones, Kate said, "I'd appreciate some water."

"I'll get it," Aimee said.

"Why don't I turn off the radio," Paula said. She rose in one fluid motion as the Pointer Sisters began to croon "Slow Hand."

Stirring in her chair, aware she was fumbling with her notebook, Kate watched Paula cross the room to a small stereo console, the slender delicate body moving in the same unified flow.

"The music you heard yesterday from Owen Sinclair's apartment," Kate said, seizing on one of the questions she must ask. "Did you notice anything special about it?"

"I never actually heard his music unless I was in the hallway." Facing Kate, Paula was silhouetted straight and slim against the sunlit window, her hands in the pockets of her chinos. "It was just noise and vibration."

"Yesterday it was *loud* noise." Aimee placed a tall glass filled with water and ice cubes on the coffee table and again sat down beside Kate. "Are you close to finding out who did this?"

"We hope to make an arrest soon." Her response was automatic. "In the meantime we need to collect all the evidence we can. Paula," she said, easing into the requirements of her job with relief, "we've learned there was an argument involving Mr. Sinclair at the party yesterday. You made no mention of it to my partner and me."

Paula, who had returned to the sofa, shrugged. "It was nothing new. The same old politics."

"What same old politics?"

She looked shrewdly at Kate. "By this time you know very well what politics."

"I'd like you to tell me."

Paula sighed. "Of course you would." She said slowly, "Owen Sinclair was an informer. Voluntarily, without coercion, he turned in his fellow citizens to a committee of witch hunters. Most decent and thoughtful people would term that despicable. But for every indefensible act, there are always defenders — like Dudley Kincaid."

"Did Mr. Sinclair name you?"

Paula's smile was wintry. "I'm sure he'd have been willing to. But he didn't know me before I moved in here."

Kate approached the subject of Paula's dead lover. "Did he name anyone you know?"

Paula shook her head. "Not that Alice and I didn't have our problems. You remember I mentioned my Alice?"

My Alice. Kate nodded.

"Alice and I were never on the blacklist, but —" She leaned forward to extinguish her cigarette. "Mildred Dunnock — do you know of her?"

"A wonderful actress," Kate offered.

"Indeed. Back then she was considered a Communist sympathizer merely because of her friendship with Arthur Miller and Lilly Hellman. My Alice was a bookkeeper, she was never in the industry, but we both had friends in common — people as liberal-minded as ourselves, some of them Communists. Alice was a friend of Paul Robeson's.

That meant trouble — harassment by the FBI. It was difficult, but at least we worked. You know, some people in this town were very angry about what was going on, and quite courageous. And some of them were famous — like Katie Hepburn, Bogie and Bacall, Gregory Peck, Burt Lancaster, Judy Garland."

Remembering the remarkable visual acuity required of Paula when she was a script supervisor, Kate said to her, "You could recall a lot of faces from those times, couldn't you."

"Thousands." Paula smiled, tapped her temple. "Memory like an elephant."

Kate got up. "Would you excuse me? I'll be just a few minutes . . ."

Downstairs in the community room, Kate washed her hands. Then she stared searchingly into the small mirror over the sink. The light blue irises of her eyes were becoming edged with red. "You look like hell," she muttered.

She rummaged in her shoulder bag for eyedrops and a comb, thinking sourly that her salt and pepper hair had more salt in it today than yesterday. But at least the grayness seemed to be adding shape and substance to the fine texture; her hair now followed a few dictates of her comb instead of falling into the same soft shapelessness as in her childhood.

She tucked her blouse more neatly into her pants and buttoned her jacket. She leaned closer to the mirror, flexing her shoulders. The jacket fit more snugly than it should. She unbuttoned it. "You're getting fat," she grumbled.

In a haze of depression she went back upstairs and into Owen Sinclair's sealed apartment. She

142

walked down the hallway into the bedroom and over to his wall of memorabilia. Ignoring the group shots from Sinclair's movies, she took all the portrait photos from the wall except for the self-identified Jack Warner, shaking off fingerprint powder as she stacked them on the dresser. After a moment's indecision, she took the photo signed *J. Parnell Thomas*. Perhaps Paula would know about him. The men in all these photos might have nothing to do with this case, but they were of obvious significance in Owen Sinclair's life, and she would find out who they were.

Back in Paula Grant's apartment, Kate said, "Sorry, these are quite dirty with fingerprint powder." She glimpsed Aimee's faint shudder.

Paula said, "Put them on the coffee table, Kate. Forgive me dear, I think of you as Kate. Do you mind?"

"Not at all." She was warm with her pleasure.

She placed the photos in a stack on the table and sat down on the sofa beside Paula as Aimee came over to sit on Kate's other side. The scent of perfume, sensual in its subtlety, reached her. She could not determine from which woman it came. She took the first photo off the stack.

"Why . . . it's Elia Kazan," Paula uttered.

Kate said, "The director of *On The Waterfront*."

"Yes . . . and many other films. He informed, he named members of his own actors' group, he named Arthur Miller, Paula Strasberg . . ."

Kate showed her the next photo.

"Budd Schulberg. Another informer. A screen-writer — he wrote *What Makes Sammy Run?* This next one . . . he's Robert Rossen, he directed *All the*

King's Men. Why . . . these men are all informers, Kate . . ."

Paula's hand went to the collar of her shirt, holding the pieces of cloth together as if to protect her throat. "Oh, God. This man is Martin Berkeley, a screenwriter . . . he was so terrible, he accused everyone, he gave the Committee over a hundred and fifty names, some of them never Communists at all . . ."

Kate held up the last photo, the one signed *J. Parnell Thomas.*

"This man . . ." Paula looked at her with appalled eyes. "The chairman of HUAC. A bully who gaveled and shouted down any witness who tried to claim any constitutional rights." Her tone turned sardonic. "A few years later he claimed the Fifth Amendment himself. He was an embezzler."

She sat tensely over the photos, staring at them, clutching the collar of her shirt. "Where exactly did you get these?"

"The wall in Mr. Sinclair's bedroom."

"That room," Paula murmured. "Truly a chamber of horrors."

From beside her Kate sensed Aimee's tremor.

"I never saw these," Paula said, "only the disgusting photo in his living room. I didn't notice anything but . . . him while I was in there."

"How could you," Aimee whispered.

"The photo in Mr. Sinclair's living room, which one was that?" Kate was ransacking her memory.

"McCarthy, of course. With his gargoyle henchman Roy Cohn. All these years it's been right on his coffee table, surely you noticed it."

Kate did not respond. There was no such photo in that apartment.

Aimee interjected, "Of all things Roy Cohn could have died from . . ."

"For years," Paula said, biting off the words, "for decades I was grateful the man denied his homosexuality. Who in our community would ever want to lay claim to a creature like him? And now he's linked to us by our worst tragedy . . ."

Easily, so easily came these admissions of community identity from Paula. Kate looked at her intently. "I take it you despise everyone who testified."

Paula shook her head. "Not at all. Some people like Lee J. Cobb were forced to inform. He was simply broken by the blacklist, it devastated his life. Sterling Hayden spent the rest of his days wandering this earth denouncing himself and what he did. Poor John Garfield — they might as well have put a gun to his head — it did kill him, you know. And Isobel Lennart, she wrote wonderful musicals for MGM — she did *Funny Girl* — she regretted informing to her dying day."

Kate wondered if Lennart had been the writer of musicals who had made it possible for Mildred Coates to practice her craft one last time.

Paula said, "I *do* despise the people who made it worse. Hedda Hopper used her column to spread the names that were named. And this man —" She pointed to the photo of Elia Kazan. "With his prestige he could have helped stop the madness. To this very day he defends what he did."

In the warmth of the apartment Paula was

rubbing her arms as if she were cold. Kate restacked the photographs, realizing that she must quickly get their contaminating presence out of this room.

In Owen Sinclair's apartment, she stared at the swirling pattern of fingerprint powder coating the coffee table as if she could divine from it, like tea leaves, the whereabouts of that photo of Joseph McCarthy and Roy Cohn.

She returned to Paula Grant's apartment. Paula was sitting with her ankles crossed, her fingers tucked over the bottom of the wine goblet she balanced in the palm of a hand. Aimee was beside her, feet curled up under her, her hair a glossy darkness against the maroon of her sweater, her eyes on Kate in a fixed stare. The women were differently attractive. But Taylor was wrong. It was Paula Grant who was beautiful.

Noticing that the dust from the photos had been expunged from the coffee table, Kate settled herself once more in her chair. She concentrated on verifying the detail of other interviews, the careful intricacies of leading Paula Grant through the events of yesterday at the party. Aimee, claiming immersion in the Dallas–Houston football game that had been on the TV in the community room, did not contribute to the conversation, but Kate was aware of her unwavering stare. Paula confirmed physical details of where Owen Sinclair had stood, and the time intervals of when others had arrived. She gave Kate names of tenants who had attended the Fourth of July party in Owen Sinclair's apartment, but she could remember nothing of significance about it.

"During the party yesterday," Kate said, "did you notice anyone leave and then return?"

"Certainly." The tone held a trace of tartness. "We were all drinking liquid of one form or another. Aimee and Houston have younger kidneys than any of the rest of us."

Kate smiled. "Do you have any idea who left when?"

Paula returned Kate's smile. "Of course not, dear." The tone was indulgent. "Who would?"

Kate looked at her watch. She regretted leaving this apartment and this woman, but leave she must. "I'm afraid I'll have further questions," she apologized to Paula.

Paula said, "We'll look forward to seeing you again."

After this Thanksgiving weekend Aimee Grant surely would return to her own place, Kate reflected.

She took one of her cards from her notebook. "If anything at all comes to mind about the case, please call me." She turned the card over and jotted her home phone number on the back. "Feel free to call me anytime."

– 14 –

Taylor flung open the door of the community room. Kate put her notes aside as he strode toward her. "News," he said, "I got news."

"About time you showed up," Hazel Turner said, following Taylor into the room. She bore a large tray with two steaming dishes.

"Hazel," Taylor said, "wait a —"

"Be quiet, you." She put down her tray and swiftly spread out place mats, napkins, cutlery, a coffee pot and mugs. Then with a flourish she served two crust-covered dishes. "Chicken pot pie," she said. "A specialty." She addressed the grinning Taylor: "A wonder it didn't dry out waiting for you to show up, buster."

"Thank you," Kate said to Hazel's back as the landlady marched out, thongs flapping. The door slammed behind her.

Chuckling, Taylor picked up his fork and broke through the crust. He inhaled deeply. "Ah, Hazel, you're a beauty," he said, digging into his food.

A rich, oniony aroma wafted to Kate. "News," she said, breaking the crust on her own dish and savoring the smell. "Fill me in."

"God, this pie is great," Taylor said, his mouth full. "I took a call for you from Joe D'Amico at the lab."

Kate looked down at her chicken pot pie to conceal a smile.

"Joe's working on some of the stuff we collected from Sinclair's apartment," Taylor continued, "those plastic bags from the trash out back. One of 'em was done up real neat, remember?"

She did. Its top had been taped securely closed. During the inspection and photography of the Beverly Malibu's dumpster, lab criminalist Napoleon Carter had taken charge, marking and booking the bag along with two others filled with party trash.

"What's in the bag is real, real interesting, Kate." Taking another mouthful of his meal, Taylor flipped open his notebook. "Get this. An eight by ten silver picture frame, the glass smashed, the photo gone. And a record album, the plastic wrapping open but still on it. Titled . . ." Taylor squinted and then

149

spelled: *"G-o-t-t-e-r-d-a-m-m-e-r-u-n-g*. And a pair of surgical gloves."

Kate, her food forgotten, was staring at him in an electricity of interest. "Surgical gloves?"

"Yeah. The album, the picture frame dusted clean. They already superglued the chair — nothing, all smudges. So we aren't gonna get prints anywhere, Kate."

"Right." She was chilled by the relentlessness, the icy premeditation of this homicide.

Taylor was grinning. He pointed his fork at her. "But our boy blew it."

Kate smiled, amused and patient, humoring Taylor and his drawing out of his news.

"Sinclair's apartment — the bathroom garbage — two unfiltered cigarette butts. Camels."

The image of Dudley Kincaid and his ceremonial smoking clear in her mind, her thoughts racing, she put down her fork. "Ed . . ."

"Yeah, and I say we put it to him." Grinning in triumph, he gestured at her lunch with his fork. "After we finish Hazel's chicken pot pie."

In one of the small, blue-walled interview rooms in Wilshire Division, Dudley Kincaid sat round-shouldered in a metal chair, his arms crossed over his gray western shirt, his eyes a blue glare through the prism of his trifocals.

In his apartment he had reacted with incredulity as Kate told him they had found discrepancies in his statements about Sinclair's death and would take him into custody for further questioning. During the half-hour drive in the Plymouth he had seethed in silence.

Taylor now said in a soothing tone, "Why don't you make this easy on everybody, Mr. Kincaid? Why don't you tell us how it happened with Sinclair?"

"You two incompetent fools are beyond all belief. A patsy, you idiots are looking —"

"We know quite a number of facts now, Mr. Kincaid," Kate interrupted, her tone conversational. "About the music, for one thing. How that was done."

"Music." Sighing in exasperation, he sat back from the formica-topped table and hooked his thumbs through his suspenders.

Taylor tilted his chair back and crossed an ankle over a knee. "You wanted him dead," he said with assurance.

Kincaid looked at him with contempt.

"We know you had your reasons," Taylor said. "Why don't you tell us about it."

Kincaid groaned in exasperation.

Kate looked over the coded notes on her yellow legal pad. She and Taylor would not mention key elements of the crime scene: the handcuffs, the subject matter of the missing photo, the type of poison used. "You removed the picture . . ." She gave him a confident look, and waited, alert but relaxed. She felt convinced from her earlier impressions of Kincaid that the man would be a clumsy liar, easy to trap in inconsistencies.

"What picture?" He was shaking his head

151

vigorously as if to unclog it of the irrationality of her words. "I don't know what the hell you're talking about."

She gave a shrug of impatience. "You're playing games. We *know* you took the picture."

He rolled his eyes toward the acoustic ceiling of the interview room.

A new angle of questioning was necessary. She said, "Tell us everything you did yesterday. From the moment you woke up."

From his shirt pocket he pulled out a crumpled half pack of Camels along with a small box of wooden matches. She watched in satisfaction this time as he went through his cigarette-lighting ceremony. If the man was a salivator, his ABO reading could be lifted from that butt and matched with the two butts found in Sinclair's apartment.

"Okay," he said, shaking out his match. "This is exactly what I did yesterday."

Even though this interview was being tape recorded, she took swift notes for her own benefit of his activities: showering, shaving, eating breakfast, working through the morning repairing a script to the accompaniment of radio talk shows, changing clothes to go down to Hazel Turner's party, returning afterward to again change clothes and continue work on the script to more radio talk shows until he was interrupted by the screams of Aimee Grant from the hallway.

She and Taylor took him twice more through these events, including close questioning of his activities at the party and the argument involving

Sinclair, but as Kincaid added more details to his increasingly impatient recital, the basic facts did not deviate. Yes, he and Sinclair had both been drinking from Sinclair's bourbon bottle during the party. No, he could not remember exactly what Sinclair had eaten — something of everything, and lots of it — but he did remember that Sinclair had lit one of his cheap cigars and had grudgingly extinguished it at the immediate howls from the women, especially Hazel Turner and Mildred Coates. Sinclair had then proceeded to mooch cigarettes from himself and Cyril Crane. Yes, people had come in and out of the community room, but none of the five involved in the argument — himself, Sinclair, Cyril Crane, Parker Thomas and Dorothy Brennan — had left.

Smoking the last two cigarettes in his pack of Camels, he insisted on relating the content of some of the radio programs he had listened to on Thanksgiving afternoon. Kate was not impressed; he could have been in Sinclair's apartment while the programs were being tape recorded in his own quarters. But she was frustrated that she and Taylor could not manage to ensnare him in any inconsistency. They seemed to be gaining no advantage in this interview.

"Mr. Kincaid," she said, deciding to play a trump card, "tell us about Jeremiah Ashton."

His reaction was gratifying: he half-rose from his chair, his jaw sagging.

"Yes," she said calmly, "we know all about him."

"Scum," he spat, "he's *scum*. Only the worst kind of Southern trash steals from his own. No better than a mongrel nigger — I said that right to his face. He's —" His face mottled, he broke off, choked by his outrage.

"They stole from you, didn't they, Dudley." Taylor's voice oozed friendliness and sympathy. "The two of them."

Kincaid clutched the edge of the table; his eyes were narrowed with pain. "Ashton was the Judas. Owen didn't have the brains to even fathom what he took. Ashton was the one who knew . . ."

Kate asked in sudden apprehension, "When was the last time you saw Jeremiah Ashton?"

The pain faded from his face. "How should I know?" His voice was low and harsh. "It's been fifteen years. I imagine he's in the Malibu beach house he bought with the blood money from *Confederate Night* and all the other screen assignments he got out of that film."

She was angry with herself over her impulsive question; Kincaid was regaining his composure.

"You hated him so much you had to kill him," Taylor said.

Kincaid turned to Kate. "This arrest smells like the doing of a woman. Unfortunately, of the two of you, it's quite obvious the male is the stupid one."

Taylor said, "What Sinclair did to you, it's been festering over the years. Isn't that right, Dudley?"

Still peering resentfully at Kate, Kincaid answered, "Of course it's festered, Bozo."

She was pleased with Taylor's composure; he too understood that Kincaid was trying to turn a common technique of interrogation on its ear. Often police interrogators played the role of good guy/bad guy, so

154

that the suspect would turn to the "good" cop for understanding and support. Kincaid was attempting to drive a wedge between herself and Taylor.

"Detective Delafield," Kincaid said, "what specious logic has your devious female mind concocted to pin this business on me?"

Watching him carefully, Kate said, "While you were in Mr. Sinclair's apartment yesterday, did you smoke?"

The glacial blue eyes behind the trifocals did not waver. "Is this a logic test? Like, while you were beheading your wife, did you wear a clean shirt?"

"Answer the question," Kate said coldly.

"I was not in his apartment," he enunciated with scorn. "Ergo, I did not smoke in his apartment."

She said with deliberate force, "We have evidence that you were in his apartment, that you smoked in his apartment."

He leaned toward her, his heavily veined hands splayed out on the formica-topped table. "I did not smoke in his apartment yesterday, I was not *in* his apartment. Perhaps you found a cigarette he mooched from me. But the more likely scenario is that this is a cheap melodramatic trick."

She matched his disdainful tone: "We don't play tricks, Mr. Kincaid, cheap or otherwise." With angry pressure on her Flair pen, she made a shorthand note on her legal pad to check whether wooden matches had also been inventoried along with the two Camels. How gratifying it would be to slam this insolent bigot behind bars.

Taylor said, "You went in there, Kincaid, and you watched him die."

Kincaid turned on him. "And how did I accomplish such a feat, you dim bulb? Did I slide in under the door?"

"You stole keys from him," Kate replied, to deflect his attention from Taylor, whose broad face was beginning to acquire color.

"Oh, I see," Kincaid said. "You two have made up facts to fit everything."

"Not quite everything," Kate replied. "We'd like you to tell us where you got the poison."

"Why, at the poison store," he said. "Listen. I'm out of cigarettes, I'm tired, I'm hungry. And this is a sick travesty."

Kate caught the gleam in Taylor's eyes. Kincaid had made a serious tactical error in his admissions.

Kincaid continued, "For what it's worth to your murky bureaucratic brains, I did not kill Owen Sinclair. I'll admit that fifteen years ago I wanted to kill him, or myself, or both. But somehow I got through it — not quite intact, my creative flow has been dammed up ever since — but I did get through it."

"We don't think so," Taylor said. "Tell us again what you did yesterday."

"This is unbelievable," muttered Kincaid, removing his glasses and rubbing his hands over his face and then back over his few strands of hair. "At least let me have some cigarettes."

"Sorry, we don't have any," Taylor said. His tone was even, but Kate heard the trace of satisfaction. "Neither my partner nor me smoke."

"How long will these questions continue?"

"Until we hear some truth. We haven't heard much truth out of you, Mr. Kincaid."

"Since I've told you everything I know," he said wearily, "then in the words of Pontius Pilate, what is truth?"

Kate replied, "Facts that add up. That make a logical pattern. Please answer Detective Taylor's question."

He slammed both fists on the table. "This is an inquisition! A baseless inquisition!"

He was tired, he was without his nicotine crutch, his nerves were being rubbed raw. She decided to goad him. "We seem to have more respect for constitutional rights than you do, Mr. Kincaid. From what you said, the suspected people hauled before Senator McCarthy's Senate Committee deserved no constitutional protection at all."

"How dare you equate me with Communists," he hissed. "With traitors trying to bring this country to its knees. With —"

"Right," Taylor said. "All we got here is a stupid little homicide."

"My *reputation*," he raged. "Do you know what this will do to my *reputation*? I don't *deserve* this."

Taylor said, "One more time, tell us what you did yesterday."

With a sigh of concession, his head down, his shoulders slumping even further, Kincaid obeyed, droning the lengthy reply. Afterward Taylor again questioned him about his activities at the party. Focusing on the interchange with difficulty, Kate took a surreptitious glance at her watch. Four twenty-five. She was tired; she had not slept since the night before last. Taylor also was looking haggard.

". . . poison," Taylor was saying. Kate jerked to attention.

Sitting up straight, Kincaid snarled, "I've told you *everything,* every goddam thing I know. If you think I've got some kind of poison pharmaceutical in my apartment, I defy you to find it. Go ahead — search my apartment, goddammit."

"You'll sign a consent form?" Kate inquired, keeping the eagerness out of her voice. A bluff, maybe he was running a bluff, and they would corner him.

He looked at her in brief, narrow-eyed scrutiny. "Yes. I can only hope it will help put an end to this. . ."

She examined her options. In a consensual search he could at any moment, even during the search, rescind his approval. Then she and Taylor would be forced to obtain an official search warrant. And while they obtained that warrant they would have to release Kincaid because they lacked sufficient evidence to hold him. And in the meantime, of course, Kincaid would destroy any evidence damaging to him. Police procedure today, Kate thought resignedly, was composed of equal parts criminal investigation and observance of legal niceties; in any major criminal trial police adherence to constitutional rights and privilege came under the closest scrutiny and challenge.

Taylor was getting to his feet. He said, "Sure can't hurt if you're telling the truth." He asked cheerfully, "How about a lie detector test?"

Kincaid got up stiffly, adjusting his bolo tie. "Detective Taylor, don't push it."

* * * * *

As Napoleon Carter and his team of criminalists meticulously examined Dudley Kincaid's apartment, Kate and Taylor alternated monitoring Kincaid for both his actions and reactions.

But after snarling, "This is like Communist Russia under Stalin," he sat at the desk near his living room window and did not even observe the search. He rolled paper into his manual typewriter and typed with two fingers in rapid, unvarying rhythm.

When Napoleon Carter asked to see the clothing Kincaid had worn to the party, he got up and went into his bedroom and mutely pointed it out. He signed with seeming indifference a consent form allowing the booking of the pants and shirt. He consented to confiscation of bottles of medication from the bathroom and foodstuffs from the kitchen. His face expressionless, he obediently chewed on a piece of gauze to contribute a saliva sample.

The team found nothing worthy of note other than a cache of pornographic magazines and tapes in the back of a file cabinet in Kincaid's bedroom. Kate, in a foreboding that toxicological tests on the contents of this apartment would reveal nothing, sat gloomily in Kincaid's living room, his unending typing wearing on her nerves. She felt him slipping past them as a suspect.

"I really ought to thank all of you goons," Kincaid told her, smiling down at his ancient Underwood as he typed. "You've broken my writer's block. I have a topic for a screenplay. The words are *flowing* out of me."

She instinctively did not want to know the topic.

"Liberal historians and writers and the liberal press have had a field day for far too long," he told her with relish. "A good, *truthful* screenplay is decades overdue. And don't think for a moment I can't get it produced."

Afterward, outside Kincaid's apartment, Kate sagged against the wall. "I've had it for now, Ed."

Her confession was one he would never make: in their unequal relationship he jealously guarded his masculine pride. His agreement took the form of a lengthy and vocal yawn. "Yeah, and we got tomorrow morning's festivities to look forward to."

Half an hour later she again walked into her apartment and gazed at the books on the coffee table, companions patiently awaiting her attention. She poured herself some scotch over ice, hoping she was not too tired to sleep, and thinking about an article she had just read in which she fit the profile of the individual most prone to problems with alcohol: a person alone, without a primary emotional relationship, and in a high-tension job.

She finished her scotch. She set her alarm and got into bed for the first time since early Thanksgiving morning, thirty-six hours ago. She slept restlessly, disturbed by kaleidoscopic images of eyes filled with blood, a child holding a pistol to her head, a woman bound and gagged with motion picture film. Toward morning she fell more deeply into sleep, the images changing into arousing visions of an elegant, aristocratic woman with confident strength in her face and her slender body.

– 15 –

The next morning she met Taylor at Wilshire
Division. They drove to USC Medical Center.

In the autopsy room, pathologists around Kate
murmured into microphones; from behind her came
the high-pitched whine of an electric saw opening a
skull. She focused on the activity directly before her,
on drawing breath entirely through her mouth, on
shutting down her sense of smell.

Pathologist Geoff Mitchell wore a plastic apron

over his khaki-gowned frame, and, in this age of AIDS, two pairs of gloves; but unlike some other pathologists in the room, no mask — he breathed through his mouth with the ease of habit.

Taylor stood beside Kate, his arms crossed over his protective gown, shifting his plastic-bootied feet as he observed along with her the activity on the stainless steel autopsy table before them. Owen Sinclair's body had been opened, and Mitchell was examining and weighing its organs as he droned into his microphone.

"Odd." The pathologist looked up, his forehead creased in fine wrinkles all the way to his hairline. "The congested viscera are totally consistent with strychnine poisoning. But there's pronounced liver degeneration, multiple hemorrhages in the loose areolar tissues, nephrosis in the kidneys."

Taylor shrugged his confusion. "Meaning what?"

"Meaning the presence of another toxic agent."

Puzzled, disconcerted by this news, Kate forgot to breathe through her mouth and almost staggered under the assault of chemicals and putrefaction from all around her. "Any idea what, Mitch?" she managed to ask.

He shook his head. "Not yet."

"Look," Taylor said, "the guy drank. Couldn't his liver —"

"Ed, there *is* a degree of fatty infiltration from alcohol abuse," Mitchell said patiently. "This degeneration is different. And specific."

"Shit," Taylor muttered. "Now what."

"We'll let you know," Mitchell said in dismissal.

Kate gave a resigned shrug. The final autopsy

results and report would be delayed — toxicological testing of tissue samples required at least two weeks.

As was her ritual after an autopsy, Kate went home for a scalding hot shower; then she inhaled pepper to induce fierce sneezing to expunge from her nasal passages the odor of the autopsy room. After a complete change of clothing she left again for the station, the windows of the Plymouth open to this unusually warm November morning.

She slowed the car on Venice Boulevard to gaze at the line of small maple trees fronting the solid sober brick of Wilshire Division, the trees echoes of her growing up years in Michigan. Except that in this anomalous climate these few puny trees were still clad in leaves of yellow-tinged flame, while Michigan's brawny maples would be bereft of foliage and collecting snowflakes. She pulled into the driveway leading to the parking lot at the rear of the station, and exchanged greetings with Sue Powell and her partner Randy Jarvis who had come in from patrol.

The Detectives Squad Room was quiet; half a dozen shirt-sleeved detectives were working the CAPs table, sifting through blizzards of paper related to Crimes Against Persons in head-down concentration. Taylor was alone in the three-team nook that housed Homicide; he sat at his desk with his elbows buried in paper, phone receiver to his ear, yawning and rubbing his eyes with a thumb and forefinger. Taking her notebook from her shoulder bag and then hanging the bag over her chair, she sat down at her desk across from him. Her own paperwork was organized, prioritized, and stacked neatly in banks of tiered files lining the back of her desk — but she still felt the familiar bone-deep weariness at the unendingness of it all.

Taylor slammed down his phone and wheeled his chair over to her, Owen Sinclair's case file in hand. "We got info over NLETS from Sinclair's FBI file, the people he named. I don't see anything there, Kate."

She nodded. "Let's go over what we do have."

He leaned back and knit his fingers together behind his head. "Trust me, it's Kincaid."

She sighed. "I want to. But if the Camel cigarettes test out, any attorney would argue they could be there from an earlier time, or been planted."

"Nap and his crew will find something."

She wished she could share his confidence. "A few things just don't add up." She flipped open her notebook. "It bothers me that we've found not a single inconsistency in Kincaid's statements."

"Kate, we know he planned this thing in detail. And we know the bastard's smart."

"Then his apartment will be clean. And he should be too smart to leave clues like cigarette butts in a trash can in the victim's apartment."

Taylor shrugged. "Even smart people do dumb things."

"Why would he take the picture, Ed? Remove it from the frame?"

He shrugged again, then grinned. "True love. We know he's a nut about McCarthy."

"So he's smart about how he talks to us and dumb about leaving cigarette butts around." She shook her head.

He said, "Do you think the holiday business is some way connected?"

She looked at him with interest. "Meaning what?"

"If Kincaid's got keys to Sinclair's apartment, why does he decide to wait and slip him the poison on Thanksgiving Day?"

"He probably didn't care what day it was. The main question is, why not simply poison him in his apartment? Why do it right out in public where he might be observed by any one of ten people?"

"Easy," Taylor said decisively. "For kicks. This whole thing was for kicks. Doing it under everybody's nose was an extra added kick."

"Ed," Kate said, "does Dudley Kincaid really strike you as the for-kicks type?"

"Anybody's the type," he said flatly.

She accepted the comment as a rebuke. "We've got a lot to do," she said, consulting the list she had made on her legal pad. "Interview Jeremiah Ashton."

"Yeah, but a waste of time," Taylor pronounced. "He ain't about to admit a thing."

"Check out the handcuffs, the stores that sell them, their sales records. The record shops — the plastic wrap being on that opera record indicates it was new. Maybe a clerk will remember selling it."

"The glamor of police work," Taylor grumbled.

"We need to talk to his ex-wives and his children. And every tenant in the Beverly Malibu we haven't talked to yet, plus reinterview the ones we've already talked to."

Taylor groaned.

Kate heard her name over the paging system. She picked up her phone. "Detective Delafield."

"Kate, Joe at the lab."

A very business-like Joe D'Amico; he was working with people all around him who did not know he was a friend of hers.

"How are you?" she said in an equally perfunctory tone.

"We've got test results you and Ed may need to know right away. Strychnine traces in bourbon, in a plastic cup from the evidence in a trash bag labeled Dumpster Party Debris. Strength point-three-zero grams. A fatal dose in anybody's textbook."

She was writing rapidly.

"Kate," he continued, "we found something else. In a Ten High bourbon bottle labeled Kitchen Counter from the victim's apartment. Arsenic trioxide. Two-point-six milligrams."

She stared sightlessly at her notebook.

"We'll notify the coroner," he said.

"The post was this morning," she said mechanically, her thoughts racing. "Do you know — never mind, I'll call Mitchell. Thanks, Joe. We appreciate it."

"Sure," he said. He added in a soft tone, "See you, dear," and hung up.

She repeated the conversation to Taylor as she dialed USC Medical Center, identified herself, and asked for Dr. Geoff Mitchell.

After only a few moments' delay Mitchell picked up the phone and said with jovial sarcasm, "I've just sewn him up and no, I don't have an answer for you yet."

"Mitch," she said urgently, "the lab's found . . ." From her notes she read him the names of the poisons and their strengths. "Could this arsenic trioxide be the other toxic agent you found?"

There was silence; she could picture his forehead creasing as he contemplated her question.

"A quantity of arsenic that small," Mitchell mused, "he'd have to take it over quite a period of time to produce organ degeneration. But —"

"Like how long?"

"Like months. But Kate, there's no evident weight loss —"

"But he did lose *some* weight in the last few months, we have statements to that effect. And if the quantity is so small that it wasn't fatal . . . Mitch, if he was ingesting this over a period of time, what would his everyday symptoms be?"

"Most likely gastritis. Nausea and diarrhea, maybe occasional vomiting. Kate, we need to look at the tissue tests —"

"Of course, Mitch. I know that. And thanks." She hung up and repeated Mitchell's statements to Taylor. "Sinclair liked to drink . . ." She was still absorbing this new information. "Before he was killed he was being poisoned, he was being tortured every single day of his life for months on end . . ."

Taylor whistled. "Christ, this one's for the psychiatry books. Kincaid must of been out of his tree over that son of a bitch."

Whoever had murdered Owen Sinclair had hated him with a pitiless savagery beyond her experience. And unless Napoleon Carter found incontrovertible evidence, the killer was not, she felt in her bones, Dudley Kincaid. But then . . . who?

– 16 –

Leaving the Station, Kate headed west over surface streets instead of taking the Santa Monica Freeway. Darkness had fallen, she was weary, and the glittering evidence in shop windows of the onrushing Christmas season depressed her. As she reviewed the five days since the autopsy of Owen Sinclair, an eye-catching luminous gold Christmas tree high on a distant office building was an annoying distraction.

An interview with Jeremiah Ashton was on hold; his housekeeper had explained in a musical Hispanic accent that the Señor had left in October for a working vacation on Crete and would return shortly after the New Year. She and Taylor would have to wait until he was back on American soil.

Sinclair's three daughters — one in New York, one in Texas, the other in Chico, California — had had minimal contact with their father over the past two decades. They expressed shock over the circumstances of his death, but little grief. "We aren't none of us close," the daughter in Chico had volunteered by phone to Kate. "I thank my savior Jesus Christ for bringing love into my life because he was an awful father. It's my Christian duty, I'll be coming down there to arrange a service — not that he'd ever thank me for it." Each of the daughters had professed ignorance of the details of his HUAC testimony, other than the controversy had blighted their childhood. "We've really tried to put all that behind us," complained the adenoidal daughter in Houston.

Of Sinclair's three ex-wives, Margaret was dead; Louise, remarried and long-since widowed, was in a convalescent hospital in Woodland Hills; and third wife Vivian shared a cramped and slovenly apartment on Cherokee in Hollywood with an elderly and crippled woman companion. Both Vivian and her roommate, Gladys, had been well on their way to beery inebriation when Kate and Taylor had arrived for an interview early Wednesday afternoon.

Vivian had professed to know little about her ex-husband's political past — "He did all that shit before my time" — or whether he had any enemies — "Yeah, plenty from years ago, but who gives a flying fuck anymore?" She was a woman with spindly arms and legs and a balloon-like body, her lined and cratered face an acid etch of her life. She asked no questions about the death of her husband of nine years; she expressed interest only in the contents of his will.

"To our knowledge," Kate informed her, "he died without one."

"Figures," Vivian had mumbled blearily, "just fucking figures. Time the lawyers get done, won't be enough for a six pack."

Kate turned her Nova, her personal car, onto La Cienega, and into more Christmas twinkle. She and Taylor had called the numbers in Sinclair's address book. The respondents had either never heard of Sinclair, or had not seen him in years. A neighborhood canvass around the Beverly Malibu had produced exactly zero. Interviews with tenants absent the day of the murder had gleaned no additional information other than useless gossip. The handcuffs used to fasten Sinclair to his death bed were a standard type sold through porn shops and theatrical supply houses; she and Taylor would have to expend shoe leather to determine if any tenant from the Beverly Malibu had patronized such a shop.

Dudley Kincaid remained their prime suspect. A positive match of his saliva sample with the Camel cigarettes in Sinclair's apartment seemed to have strengthened their case, but a subsequent interview with him had diminished the evidentiary value of their finding. He had smoked in Sinclair's apartment on a number of recent occasions, he contended; just the week before, in fact, he'd been in there to give Sinclair a brochure he had obtained through a KIEV radio program, *The Voice of Americanism*. The pamphlet should still be in the apartment. And it was: *How the Reds are Re-invading Hollywood,* buried in a magazine rack in the living room.

If she found it difficult to wholeheartedly commit herself to Kincaid as their prime suspect, she could come up with no better alternative. Of the tenants at that Thanksgiving Day party with access to Sinclair, what provable motivation for murder could be ascribed to landlady Hazel Turner? To aged film editor Mildred Coates? To actress Maxine Marlowe? Actor Cyril Crane? Historian Parker Thomas? Paula Grant?

Dorothy Brennan, relatively new to the Beverly Malibu, was an unknown quantity, and with more concrete details of her past gleaned from a second interview they had obtained a copy of her employment application from Dayton Room Dividers, her last employer. The details on that application checked out well enough: she had lived at the same address in Silverlake for the past fourteen years, had been widowed in 1974, and had held a series of office jobs.

And as for Paula Grant . . . Kate was on her way now to see her. She had not called to announce herself; she had not known that she would call on her until she had stepped into her car this evening in the parking lot at Wilshire Division.

Hazel Turner was outside the Beverly Malibu standing in a tiny puddle of light cast from a bulb over the doorway, harvesting a bloom from the two bushes of bird of paradise. She clutched the sleeve of Kate's jacket. "We need to know what's going on. Is Dudley the one? Is that why you took him in? Why aren't you keeping him there?"

Kate tried to soothe her urgency. "We're still investigating, Hazel. We can't arrest anyone unless we have enough evidence."

"Only as it should be," Hazel said. "But everybody's plenty nervous, don't you know."

"Yes," Kate said with sympathy. "We're doing our best."

She walked down the second floor hall to Paula Grant's apartment, hesitated, and then continued on to Owen Sinclair's apartment, staring at the police seal across the door as if she could divine something from it. She returned to Paula Grant's apartment, straightened her jacket, then rang the doorbell.

Moments went by, stretching on and on. Then a voice that did not sound like Paula's: "Yes?"

"It's Kate. Kate Delafield."

There was the scrape of a deadbolt being withdrawn, and then Paula Grant was looking at her with a perfunctory smile, her gaze fixed on some distance beyond Kate. Her slender, elegant body was clad in a long cream-colored silk kimono tied with a sash the color of jade.

In confusion Kate stammered, "I'm so sorry . . ." She felt light-headed, disoriented.

"Come in, my dear," Paula said with a velvety softness Kate had never heard in her low tones. A cool hand took Kate's hand and drew her in.

Kate entered a darkened living room smelling of

lavender and candle wax. On the coffee table a circle of lighted, flickering tapers in crystal holders surrounded a careful arrangement of photographs and two tall-stemmed, silver wine glasses.

The candles, the photographs, the wine, the robe. A ceremony. She was intruding on some sort of intensely private ceremony.

"Call, I should have called," Kate stumbled over the words. She felt no less an intruder than if she were a burglar.

"It's quite all right," Paula said in the velvet voice. "I knew you would understand or I would never have answered the door. Sit there." She gestured to the sofa, in front of the circle of candles, the photos, the wine.

Kate did not want to be here. Gingerly, not knowing what else to do with herself, she sat down where she was told. Unwillingly, she stole a glance at the photos. They were all of the same curly-headed blonde woman at various ages, from the teens into perhaps late fifties.

"My Alice," Paula said. "Today is . . . an anniversary."

"I see," Kate managed.

"She's been gone five years now."

Kate nodded. As had her Anne.

"We were first for each other." Paula's voice had lowered to a whisper. "There was no one before her. She was the only one, ever, for me."

Kate had put away the things of Anne. She was recovering from Anne, learning to live without Anne.

She did not speak; Paula did not want a colloquy, she wanted to talk.

"I was first and only for Alice, too," Paula said. "Like swans, we mated for life. Forever. Like swans."

Kate started to get up. She had to get out of here. Now.

Paula, sitting beside her, said, "You have important questions, I know. I understand and so would Alice. How can I help you, dear?"

To business. Yes, to the business she had used as an excuse to come here. She pulled a photocopy of a computer printout from her shoulder bag. She said with difficulty, "This list is . . . these are the people Owen Sinclair named. Do you recognize anyone?"

Paula spread the paper over the coffee table, smoothing it under one of the flickering tapers. The finger she ran down the list cast a wavering shadow.

"Dear, dear Sam Ornitz," she murmured. "And yes, Lester Cole. Adrian Scott . . . Ring Lardner, Jr. . . . Dalton Trumbo . . . Kate, these first five are members of the Hollywood Ten — they went to jail for defying HUAC."

Kate nodded. This identifying tag had come in with the FBI report. She felt a welling of tears in her throat, and swallowed.

"John Garfield of course you know. And the actress Gail Sondergaard. And Howard Da Silva. David Lang was a cartoonist. Marguerite Roberts is a screenwriter, she's on in years and quite ill, living in Santa Barbara the last I heard . . ."

Along with Paula, Kate looked over the remaining names:

John Robert Campbell
Randall Marlowe Reese
Alistair Todd Smythe
Gillian Anne Smythe
Martin Brooks Smythe
Meaghan Dorothea Smythe
Robert Michael Tonelli
Louise Brenda Tonelli

"Alistair Smythe rings a bell," Paula offered. "None of the other names do."

"He was identified to us as an actor."

"Ah. Yes. But a theatrical actor. A protege of Chaplin's. I believe Alistair Smythe had his own Hollywood theater group back in the fifties."

"Thank you," Kate said, quickly rising. "I'm very sorry to disturb you." Finally she could escape this apartment, and this woman, whose life had no possible place for her.

Paula showed her to the door. As she turned to bid Paula good night, Kate knew from Paula's eyes that she had not truly registered Kate's presence.

She drove swiftly down Wilshire Boulevard through Beverly Hills. The street lights were decorated with panels of pine trees and reindeer; across the Boulevard were stretched illuminated, blinking depictions of snowmen and ice dancers, with smoke billowing from Christmas chimneys.

The worst day of her life by far, she reflected, had been the day she had buried Anne, the day when

Anne was finally gone. But this evening was somewhere in there with the other kinds of worst.

— 17 —

Kate closed her apartment door and for a moment leaned a hand against it. Dropping her mail uninspected onto the coffee table, she went into the bedroom to change into a pair of wash-softened jeans and a loose-knit sweater.

She glanced apathetically over the frozen dinners in her freezer and pulled out a tray of ice cubes. She would have a scotch, put on some music, and then think about eating. Lena Horne, this was a Lena Horne evening.

The buzzer sounded.

She looked at her watch: seven-fifty. A Jehovah Witness? Another kid soliciting newspaper subscriptions? She pressed the listening device on her intercom. "Yes?"

"It's Aimee Grant. Could I please see you for a few minutes?"

Aimee Grant? How on earth . . . Kate buzzed her in.

The young woman wore a dark brown soft leather jacket with oversize shoulder pads, and loose-fitting black pants tucked into ankle-high boots. Standing in the apartment doorway, she seemed even younger than Kate's memory of her.

"Sorry to bother you." The glance darted everywhere except at Kate's face.

"No problem." Kate stood aside to allow her entry. "How did you find out where I live?"

Aimee shrugged. "You left your home phone number with my aunt." She looked sheepish. "I work for a law firm, I checked the cross-listing of phone numbers with addresses. Then I came over here and looked at the mailboxes."

Kate nodded. So easily was privacy defeated these days. She did not inquire why Aimee Grant had not simply phoned; she herself had not phoned Paula Grant earlier this evening. Perhaps, like herself, Aimee had wanted face-to-face contact; she had not wanted to risk being turned away with just a phone call. "Sit down," she said in welcoming warmth. Aimee's visit would not end in a disaster similar to her own intrusion on Paula Grant.

"Neat digs," Aimee offered. "I like all the wood."

"Thanks." She could not remember the last time anyone had visited her in this apartment. "I was

179

fixing myself a scotch. Would you join me? It's all I can offer at the moment."

"Sure."

"With water?"

"Whatever you're having."

When Kate returned, Aimee had dropped her jacket into a chair and was kneeling to examine a tape from Kate's music collection. Kate stared at the blue pullover Aimee wore, an unbidden image insinuating itself into her mind — the slender austerity of Paula Grant's body. Aimee's body in its ripe youthfulness was unlike Paula's . . . except for the straight set of those shoulders . . .

"Keely Smith," Aimee said. "Good songs on here but I don't know her." She returned the tape to its slot and wandered, head down, in a circuitous path to where Kate sat on the sofa. She held her scotch in both hands, looking at it, then took a sip. Her expression did not change, but her faint shudder was visible.

Kate smiled. "Maybe you'd prefer scotch and water and hold the scotch."

Aimee finally met Kate's eyes. "You have a terrific smile, you know." Her own lips were narrowed with tension. "I really don't need anything to drink."

What did Aimee Grant want? Why had she come here? "You live around here, don't you?" Kate said, to try to put her at ease.

"Brentwood." Aimee gestured vaguely. "Three of us have a condo. The only way to afford the rent."

Kate nodded encouragingly. This young woman,

for whatever reason she was here, was a welcome distraction. "Who's the three of us?"

"Cheryl and Jennifer. Joanie took off." She picked up one of the books Joe D'Amico had loaned Kate and examined it. Replacing the book, she flicked hair back from her face with a shake of her head, met Kate's eyes and then looked away. "We were lovers till I found out she was shooting up. You don't mind me telling you this, do you?"

Kate shook her head. "Not at all."

"You being a cop and all . . . I can't tell my aunt any of this stuff. Joanie injected the junk in different places so I couldn't tell."

"Yes. Some dopers do that."

"And the way she acted sometimes . . . I thought she was just moody." She shrugged. "Stupid me."

"Not really. Dopers learn how to fool people that way, too."

"Yeah, well, I found out she'd slept with a million people, men even. I took an AIDS test. Ever wait out an AIDS test?"

"No. But I know people who have."

"You sure you're safe? Lots of us are just kidding ourselves."

"I'm not kidding myself," she said evenly. Safety was the sole benefit of her arid emotional life of these recent years.

Aimee's smooth face seemed suddenly shadowed with incipient lines. "I can't stand knowing I'm going to lose people I care about. I can hardly stand being around Houston."

Kate managed to conceal her surprise and dismay.

"All those brains," Aimee said, "not to mention good looks. It's not right. Or fair. Do you know he's a scientist at Cal Tech?"

Remembering the extreme thinness of the young black man, his gallant dignity, Kate shook her head. "How is he doing?"

"Better. He's had bouts with pneumonia, but he's on medication that really seems to be helping."

"And Cyril Crane, he's . . . all right." She managed to turn the words into a statement, of hope.

"Seems to be. I like Mr. Crane a lot."

Kate nodded. She did as well.

Then Aimee looked at her. Kate was caught by the defenselessness in blue-violet eyes that were the same shape, she suddenly realized, as Paula Grant's.

"Help me, please," Aimee whispered. "That dead guy . . . all the time I see his face. I can't sleep unless I drop a 'lude — I'm sorry, I know you're a cop but it's the only way I can get him out of my head for a while." Aimee's voice was barely audible. "You saw him too. That face, those eyes all blood . . . and you did more than just see him. I need to know, it's important . . . How can you . . . Why do what you do?"

Kate felt a perilous shift in her defenses. She picked up her scotch and then put it back down, knowing that its hot strength would weaken her further.

"I started my police career in Juvenile," she began, and then the words seemed to pour from her. "I saw broken children, youngsters twisted and crippled by their lives, I heard so many terrible stories, I saw so much pain . . . and finally I felt . . . helpless to fix anything."

"If I were one of those kids," Aimee offered softly, "I'd be grateful for a woman cop like you."

Kate shook her head. "I don't know. Some police officers are wonderful with kids — they don't seem to feel nearly as inadequate as I did. Aimee, I met an assault victim on the street the other day . . . She was raped in a street attack about seven years ago, when she was fourteen. On the scale of such things, her attacker was a 'gentle' rapist. I did what I could to take care of her, but Francine still had that same . . . haunted look I saw the night of the attack."

She knew she could not find words capable of describing those empty dark eyes like blasted craters she had seen in Vietnam. And her own desolate conviction that Francine Pritchett would carry that emptiness to the grave. "She made me understand again why I belong in homicide. Homicide victims don't hurt. The dead can't tell me what it all means to them — and I can't do the wrong thing to them. Aimee . . . maybe it will help if you remember that whatever Owen Sinclair looked like, whatever he endured, at least when you and I saw him it was over. There was nothing on earth we could do."

Aimee sighed and nodded. "Except," she said, "except you can find out who's responsible."

"Yes." She picked up her scotch, sipped from it. That the heat would open her wider was something she suddenly needed. "A homicide victim is bearable for me to look at because it's clear and precise what my duty is. To do what I can to guard the last elements of that person's dignity, to protect, even in death, that person's rights. To search for Owen Sinclair's killer no matter how much effort it takes, no matter how long it takes."

"Detective Delafield," Aimee said as if she were examining each syllable. "You're very unusual."

Unsettled by Aimee's direct gaze, her transparent admiration, Kate needed to deflect attention from herself. "What do you do for your law firm?"

"I'm a paralegal. It's entertainment law."

"Sounds interesting," Kate said, her voice seeming to come from somewhere outside herself. She sipped her scotch.

Aimee was speaking, but Kate had difficulty concentrating on the words. Her eyes had fixed on Aimee's hands. She remembered her first interview with Paula, her awareness then that Aimee's hands were the same long slender shape as Paula's. She remembered the coolness of the hand that earlier this evening had taken hers and drawn her into that shrine to another woman.

". . . review contracts and research clauses . . ."

Kate forced herself to look up. The glitter of two small diamonds, in delicate earlobes almost hidden by Aimee's dark hair, caught her eyes. The bearing of Aimee's head was like Paula's. The curve of her lips.

". . . agents and accountants for some pretty big names like . . ."

The patrician nose. The straight, brush-stroke eyebrows. The fine texture of the hair. The throat with its firm, tight flesh.

Kate stared down at the drink in her hand. Was

there to be no escape from Paula? Even the soft voice held inflections, echoes of Paula's voice.

This was crazy. Three years ago she had been attracted to a woman she had thought resembled Anne — and of course Ellen O'Neill hadn't resembled her at all. Why was she going through this irrationality again? What in God's name was the matter with her? Words from a half-forgotten song floated through her head, something about not being with the one you love, so you love the one you're with. Kate bowed her head, closed her eyes.

She realized that Aimee had gotten up.

"Guess you've had a rough day. Sorry I imposed." Aimee was picking up her jacket, Aimee was leaving.

She couldn't leave. Kate was not yet ready to have her leave, to be alone again. She followed Aimee to the door, searching for a way to make her stay.

Aimee turned to her. Kate felt hypnotized by her eyes, the depth and beauty of their color. *She's beautiful,* she realized with shock.

Aimee's hand took hers. Aimee's hand, that was like Paula Grant's hand. But warm. So warm . . .

"Thank you," the young woman murmured. "It helped me to be here . . ."

She draped her jacket around her shoulders and then embraced Kate. "Thank you," she repeated. "You're so —"

The warmth, the ripeness of Aimee's body instantly permeated her. She took Aimee in her arms. Eyes squeezed shut, she pressed her cheek against Aimee's face and inhaled sweet fragrance from her hair. She brushed her lips across the fine smooth skin over the cheekbones. Her arms tightened.

Aimee gripped her arms, pulling them away. Looking into Kate's face with eyes rounded in pure astonishment, Aimee reached behind her, fumbled at the door, opened it, and was gone.

– 18 –

Kate slid her living room window open and stared bleakly into the bushy blue-green needles of the scotch pine outside her second-story apartment. The tree had been the amenity that persuaded her to lease this apartment: the spreading crown of evergreen branches shielding her from the adjacent apartment building evoked her native Michigan. In fog or rain she could smell the earthy pine scent.

She listened for the slam of a car door, an engine exploding to life, the shrieking tires of the car roaring away. But there was only the customary ocean-like

whish of traffic moving down Montana Avenue, the
rhythmic screek of crickets, the chirping of a lone
nocturnal mockingbird, and from a nearby apartment
the faint sound of Nat King Cole singing "The
Christmas Song."

Everything she had done tonight had been a
blunder, a disaster. Numb with misery, she leaned on
the windowsill, unable to turn and look into her
empty apartment.

The buzzer sounded.

Like an automaton she walked to the intercom
and pushed the front door release, then waited, her
mind frozen, for the knock.

Aimee, her jacket slung over one shoulder, closed
the door behind her. She dropped the jacket onto the
floor.

"I didn't think you knew I was alive," she said
quietly. "I'm crazy attracted to you, but that's not
why I came here tonight. So I needed a few minutes.
To . . . change gears."

She stared into Kate's eyes, the blue-violet eyes
coming ever nearer, her hands slowly sliding up
Kate's arms.

Then Aimee's face was pressed between Kate's
shoulder and her neck; Kate buried her own face in
the fragrant softness of Aimee's hair. Kate was braced
up against the door and pulling Aimee closely into
her, the warmth of Aimee's body producing heat at a
wildly exponential rate in her own body.

Aimee took Kate's face between her hands,
Aimee's mouth came to hers in tender sweetness.
Kate could not make herself be gentle; her arms
tightened around Aimee's back and hips, pressing
Aimee's body, her thighs, into hers. Aimee's mouth

became possessive; her tongue brought surges of desire, keenly specific heat to Kate's legs, the tongue-strokes creating astonishing weakness.

Aimee slid her hands under Kate's sweater. She cupped a breast, her palm sliding across the nipple. She took her mouth away from Kate's. "Shouldn't we go to bed," she said, not a question.

Aimee kicked off her boots and discarded clothing as she went down the hall. In Kate's darkened bedroom she stripped off Kate's clothing. Her hands on Kate's shoulders, she backed Kate onto the bed, lowered her naked body onto hers.

Kate knew she should assert herself with this woman who had assumed control of her. But some entity had taken possession of her body, had rendered it helpless under the sensuous body in her arms, the unutterable softness of the breasts melding with hers, the velvet thigh nestled between her legs, the voluptuous mouth on hers, the tongue that sweetly stroked ever more helplessness into her.

A woman had never done this to her first, she thought dimly some time later, groaning with her sensation as Aimee's hand cupped between her legs, as Aimee's fingers found her and began unhurried stroking. Never, she never came first with a woman. But her hips were rocking with increasing intensity under those fingers, and orgasm was taking molten shape within her.

Afterward, Aimee's body again lay on hers; the soft dark triangle Kate had managed to only briefly touch was fastened between her legs. Aimee's hands clasped Kate's breasts, her breath came in gasps as her hips rode back and forth, her buttocks firm with tension under Kate's hands.

This was a way she had always before pleased herself after she had brought a woman to orgasm . . .

Aimee's hips thrust urgently, then stilled. Then her body became a melting, spreading softness on Kate as she collapsed, moaning her gratification, her hair a sweeping silkiness across Kate's cheek as she buried her face on the pillow above Kate's shoulder.

Kate tightened her arms around her, her own breathing ragged with arousal from the prolonged erotic friction between her legs. With a throaty murmur of pleasure, Aimee brought her mouth to Kate's breasts. Soon, her hand came to Kate's legs. As it would again and again that night.

In the early morning darkness, Kate disentangled herself from the silken warmth of Aimee's sleeping body. She went into the bathroom, into the shower. The cool water that sluiced over her seemed ineffectual on her heated skin. Her breasts felt swollen and heavy, the dull sweet ache in her nipples an echo of the savoring they had received throughout the night.

Never before had a woman taken such endless delight in her breasts. Never before had she known such orgasmic rapture throughout a night. Never had she suspected that she could. Or that she would ever want to. Or need to. Even after all that, she still felt vaguely aroused. There had been too many "never befores" during this night. Fastening the towel around her, Kate returned to the bedroom.

Aimee was awake; she lay looking at Kate, her hair dishevelled darkness against the pillowcase. She sat up and shook her hair back from her face and gazed at Kate, holding the sheet modestly above her breasts, her eyes wanton.

"Come here for a minute."

"I have to get ready for work," Kate said, scarcely recognizing her own voice.

"I know," Aimee said. She tossed the sheet away.

Kate moved toward the bed as if under hypnotic command, needle-sharp sensation in her nipples, her arousal a swelling urgency.

Aimee sat on the side of the bed. She unfastened the towel; it fell to the floor. She slid from the bed to kneel on the carpet. Her warm hands clasped Kate's hips.

"What do you taste like," she said, not a question.

Aimee's mouth was weakening her knees; Kate pressed them into the side of the bed, a hand grasping the headboard for support. Trembling everywhere, she flung her head back. *I never come from this . . .*

The phone on the nightstand shrilled.

She knew she must answer, but only a pause in the paralyzing strokes of Aimee's tongue made it possible. She took Aimee's head in her hands, pulled her mouth away.

"Don't answer," Aimee groaned.

Kate stumbled the one step to the nightstand, picked up the phone, discovered that she had no voice.

"Kate? Kate, are you there?"

She recognized Lieutenant Rodriguez, the watch commander. "Yes," she croaked. She cleared her throat. "Yes, Lieutenant."

"Kate, are you okay?"

"Fine. Maybe . . . a touch of laryngitis." She did not dare look at Aimee, who now sat on the bed.

"We need you and Ed at a fatal accident, Olympic and Fairfax."

"Yes, sir. Right away."

She hung up, and leaned over in prickling self-consciousness to pick up the towel. Not looking at Aimee, she backed away from the bed, over to her dresser. "I have to leave. Immediately."

"So I gather. Do I?"

"You?" she said in confusion. "Don't you need to go to work?"

"At nine."

Now in panties and a bra, Kate felt somehow more protected, but not enough. Her sexual defenselessness with Aimee Grant was beyond comprehension. But at least her wits were returning. She moved to the closet, blindly yanked a pair of pants from a hanger and pulled them on.

Aimee rose and came toward her, the sensuous young body palely glowing. She kissed her on the cheek. "Good morning." She walked past her into the bathroom.

Kate leaned against the folding doors of her closet, her mind and body in a maelstrom.

She finished dressing; Aimee had still not emerged from the bathroom. She tapped on the door. "Just let yourself out, okay?"

"Okay. You going to be here tonight?"

"Yes." When nothing further was forthcoming, Kate said, "Have coffee, whatever you want. Leave your number and I'll call you, okay?"

"Okay."

Kate fled.

The day passed strangely. Part of herself dwelt on the night's extraordinary sexuality; the other part watched in dispassion as she performed her work with competence and exactness.

The accident fatality had been a young Hispanic male, his Corvair broadsided by a Ford Bronco, its driver a beefy young man nearly comatose with drug intoxication. The glove compartment of the truck had been stuffed with packets of crack. Her morning and part of the afternoon had been occupied with taking statements from witnesses at the scene, and booking the suspect for DUI, felony manslaughter, felony possession with intent to distribute. Later that afternoon she and Taylor, using snapshots Hazel had given them of tenants at earlier parties, had continued their survey of more porno shops that sold handcuffs like those used on Owen Sinclair.

She entered her apartment. A piece of notepaper on the coffee table contained a phone number written in large bold numerals. Kate walked into the kitchen, looking around curiously. If Aimee had eaten or drunk anything, it was not apparent. She herself had not eaten last night nor today. Taylor, clucking sympathy at her uncharacteristic choice of iced tea for lunch, was convinced she must have a flu virus ready to hatch.

She walked into the bedroom, and smiled at the made bed. The scene of last night's passion made innocent, pristine.

Images that could not be made pristine intruded into her mind: this morning's accident victim crushed by a car door crimson with blood and shredded flesh. She needed a shower. Before anything else she needed a shower.

Afterward she tied a terrycloth robe around her, thinking that her breasts still seemed slightly swollen. But then she still felt arousal, like a thrumming within her that had not ceased since last night. She went into the kitchen to fix herself a scotch before calling Aimee.

The buzzer sounded.

Surely it wasn't . . . She flipped on the intercom. "Yes?"

"Hi. It's me."

Aimee, again wearing the leather jacket, holding a bag of groceries, brushed past Kate and went on into the kitchen.

"I thought I'd make us dinner." She opened the refrigerator. "You ought to throw this crap away. The way you eat is terrible."

Kate, arms crossed, leaned back against the cupboards and watched, entertained, as Aimee quickly unpacked pasta, hamburger, cans of sauce, french bread, a large bottle of seltzer. The young woman was amazingly beautiful. And equally amazing was the fact that Taylor had seen it before she. But of course she had been focused on Paula. And yes, the two women *did* resemble each other . . .

Finished with her work, Aimee turned to Kate and boldly inspected her as she slipped out of the leather jacket. Kate felt suddenly vulnerable, acutely conscious of her nakedness under the robe, and of the thrumming that now had considerably heightened in pitch.

Aimee tossed her jacket aside. Half-smiling, she ran her fingers through Kate's hair. "I do like wet hair."

Her hands came to Kate's shoulders, then to the lapels of Kate's robe. "Terrycloth, too."

Unsmiling, she looked into Kate's eyes as she slid her warm hands inside the robe and down over Kate's breasts.

She untied the belt, parted the robe. Then brought the palms of her hands to her mouth to moisten them, then back to Kate's breasts, the palms sliding over the nipples. Her mouth came to Kate's.

Much later, with Kate's body a turmoil of arousal under her hands, she took her mouth away. "Don't you want me to finish what we were doing this morning," she said, not a question. She knelt.

Kate's breathing became rasps. She gripped the sides of counter top for support. Like this morning, each tongue-stroke intensified her sensation, but swept strength from her knees. She reached blindly backward and seized the handle of a cabinet door above her. Paralyzed, hovering endlessly on the edge of orgasm, desperate for the release that eluded her, she could not use her hands to direct Aimee's head. She was forced to gasp her need: "Higher . . . there. Faster . . ." She tensed, quivering, arched in rapture. She heard — felt — a sound of ecstasy from Aimee's throat.

Aimee wiped her mouth on Kate's robe. She got up, her eyes heavy-lidded, her face flushed, and closed Kate's robe and tied it.

"Are you hungry right now?" she asked.

Kate unpried her hand from the cabinet handle, her breath slowing, strength seeping back into her legs. "No," she managed to say. "Are you?" She reached for a paper towel; she was incredibly wet.

"Yes. For more of what I just had." Aimee took the paper towel from her. "I want you wet." She held the ends of Kate's belt in a hand. "Let's go to bed, okay?" she said, not a question. Taking the ends of the belt in one hand, she led Kate from the kitchen.

In the bedroom, her naked body covering Kate, she began lengthy deep kissing. Soft sounds coming from her, she rotated and then thrust passionately in the wetness between Kate's legs. Afterward she got a towel and gently dried Kate.

Her mouth made Kate very wet again; and again she lay in the wetness in an intense, prolonged connection of their bodies that Kate wanted never to end.

– 19 –

The shout of "It's open!" greeted Kate's knock.

With a disapproving sigh, Kate entered Maggie Schaeffer's house, locking the door behind her. How many times had she lectured Maggie on her carelessness about her personal safety?

Maggie was seated on the hearth of her blazing fireplace, a huge ceramic mug cradled between her hands. The smell of coffee and toast permeated the house. "Shitty weather," she growled.

On this weekday morning she wore faded green sweat pants and a gray sweatshirt, concessions to the

the uncharacteristically cold temperatures invading Southern California. Kate could not remember having seen Maggie in clothing other than cotton pants or shorts, and T-shirts emblazoned with such messages as LORD LOVE A DYKE. She lived in the San Fernando Valley because she thrived in the hot summers, and she had managed to buy this one-bedroom stucco on a decaying street in Pacoima, the property's major asset a large backyard, its tiny swimming pool adorned by a wide handsome deck; she had added a brick barbecue which she used the two weeknights when she was not running the Nightwood Bar.

Her gaze sharpened on Kate but her voice was soft: "Where's the rest of you?"

Kate grinned. She had never become accustomed to the gentle feminine voice issuing from Maggie's weathered face and burly body. "I've lost a little weight," she conceded. In the ten days since Aimee had first come to the apartment, she had lost eight pounds.

"Gain it back, you look better. Who wants a scrawny cop? There's coffee and toasted bagels and cream cheese in the kitchen. Take extra cream cheese," she added as Kate, chuckling, made her way into the minuscule kitchen.

"So how are things at the Nightwood Bar?" Kate inquired as she eased herself, coffee and bagel in hand, into the comfort of Maggie's roomy couch.

Maggie extended her hands to the fire and chaffed them. "Last night Patton decided we had to vote for the most popular song on the jukebox. So she collects napkin votes and it turns out to be the Shirelles. So then she decides we have to do a sing-along. She

198

divides the bar into sections for harmony, even has five women singing the sha-la-la." Maggie lit an unfiltered Pall Mall. "You haven't lived till you've heard thirty-five dykes wailing *Will You Still Love Me Tomorrow?*"

Laughing, Kate said, "Sorry I missed it."

"Me too. Where you been lately?"

Immediately sobered by the business of this visit, Kate said, "Well, I met somebody."

Maggie's swift grin faded as she contemplated Kate. "Why do I get the feeling this is good news and bad news?"

"She's a *kid*, Maggie," she said, shaking her head. "A baby. I have no business being involved with her, I can't understand how this happened. Or how to get myself out of it."

Her thatch of whitish hair wreathed in the smoke of her Pall Mall, her tanned face expressionless, Maggie asked, "How old is she?"

"Twenty-five."

"Oh for chrissakes, Kate," Maggie uttered in disgust, flicking ash into the fireplace. "I thought she was twelve."

"Twenty-five is bad enough," Kate said morosely, putting her bagel on the coffee table and slouching down into the couch.

"You actually think that's *young*?"

"Come on, Maggie. Think about it. Where was she when Kennedy was shot? She was born a month before. When Bobby Kennedy died she was five years old. History to her is Chernobyl. The Challenger explosion."

"Lucky her," Maggie muttered. Turning her back to the fire, she stretched her legs straight out on the worn yellow-brown carpet. "What do you want, she should live through Hiroshima? Auschwitz?"

Kate said, "I have no business being involved with a witness in a capital murder case."

Maggie shrugged. "Ain't life a bitch. If you'd get around a little more you wouldn't be restricted to meeting women at your murder scenes."

Kate sighed. "Maggie, I need to figure out why I can't . . . let go of this."

"Why do you want to?"

"She's a kid," Kate repeated, disheartened. She had come here out of the conviction that she must talk to this woman whose intelligence and perspective she trusted, this woman who had become, over the past two and a half years, her friend.

"What does she do for a living?"

"She's a paralegal. In Century City."

"Doesn't sound very kid-like. And it gives you something in common with her, doesn't it? Allied professions."

Kate shook her head. "It's entertainment law. And you know I can't talk about my work. How can I talk about what I do?" She picked up her coffee, sipped from it, then deeply inhaled its odor. Yesterday she and Taylor had entered a ransacked apartment on Hauser where an elderly occupant lay beaten to death, his body across his hot plate, his chest virtually cooked by one of the electric burners. She could still smell the stench. "Nobody can understand except another cop."

"That's what *you* think," Maggie said unsympathetically. "Surely the two of you talk?"

"We talk," Kate said. She fidgeted on the couch. "But . . . not much."

"Ah. Now I understand the weight loss. Katie, you better move your stove and refrigerator into the bedroom. Or a cot into the kitchen."

Annoyed by Maggie's levity, Kate took another swallow of coffee that was as strong and hot as station house brew.

Maggie asked, "Do you talk between orgasms? Or does she lie there and play with her rattle?"

"Dammit, stop laughing at me."

"Do I look like I'm laughing?" Maggie said, rubbing a hand over her chin. "I'm just trying to figure out why you're upset about this."

"I don't know what she sees in me," Kate said.

Maggie sighed. "Of course you don't. It's part of your charm."

Hunching over and staring into her coffee mug, Kate said, "I don't do much self-analysis, Maggie. It takes away my ability to function. I can't afford to think about . . . some things." She continued musingly, "But I wonder if my work has something to do with all this, with Aimee. My whole life's been involved with death. First, my parents' deaths. Vietnam. Then —"

"What about Vietnam? Why don't you ever talk about that?"

"I'm not ready to," Kate said evenly. "There are whole periods in your own life you don't talk about, either."

Maggie waved a hand. "Go on."

"Then there was Anne. It's been five years and two months since she died, and it's still . . ." She shrugged. There was no describing this chasm in her life covered only by the thinnest of membranes. "And there's my work — every day I'm in the death

201

business. And there's my age. Is it because I've been around death so much that I've become obsessed with so young a woman? Maybe . . ."

Kate paused, thinking: But how does any of this explain my feeling for Paula Grant, who's many years closer to death than I am? But she did not intend to talk about Paula Grant.

She said, "Maybe I've got this thing about Aimee because subconsciously I know I'm running less risk of losing her to death."

"Listen to yourself, Kate." Maggie's tone was brusque. "Does all this mean you never get to smile again? Have fun? If life is so goddam grim, why don't you just get in the cell with your criminals?"

Kate sipped her coffee, reflecting over these words, knowing Maggie was not finished.

Maggie said, "Everything you mentioned is a reason. But I still don't see a problem. Okay, so she's fifteen or so years younger than you. So what?"

"She's . . ." Kate hesitated, discarding several possible words, and then uttered, "She's *aggressive*."

"Ah," Maggie said.

"She's . . . not my style," Kate mumbled. "Women like her . . . have never been my style. I don't know why she's turned me into a . . . I don't know what's the matter with me."

Her tension easing somewhat now that she had broached the true problem, Kate put a foot up on a mushroom-shaped ottoman.

Maggie's hooded dark eyes inspected her through clouds of cigarette smoke. "What's she like?"

"She's young."

Maggie cast her a glare of exasperation. "What are her interests?"

"She's quite a reader, non-fiction mostly, on all different kinds of subjects. She loves music."

"Well, that's good. You do too."

"Yes, well, I like people like Ella and Sarah. She likes U2 and Guns 'n Roses."

"A healthy young woman who likes the best of what's current," Maggie said. "Don't be an old stick-in-the-mud, Kate."

"She plays the tapes. I don't mind them. She likes sports. Especially golf."

"Golf? She likes the dumb game that old white men play?"

"No, the dumb game that attractive young women play. She's an avid follower of the women's tour."

Maggie shrugged noncommittally. "Yeah, the dykes in the bar always watch when it's on TV. What does she look like?"

"Brunette. Eyes the color of Elizabeth Taylor's." Kate said unhappily, "She's drop-dead gorgeous."

"Gee, I'm sorry, Kate. What a damn shame."

"It's not funny, Maggie. I feel like I'm not a sane woman around her. She . . . she . . ." She could not bring herself to further explain her entrapment in Aimee's sexual magnetism. She reached into her shoulder bag for her wallet, and the photo Aimee had given her. She handed it to Maggie.

"Jesus," Maggie breathed. "She looks like a brunette Candice Bergen."

"She does *not*," Kate snapped.

Maggie stared at her over the photo. "Pardon me all to hell for so horrendous an insult."

"It's what my partner says about her," Kate muttered.

"Well, far be it from me to agree with the

203

block-headed Detective Taylor." Maggie handed back the photo. "She doesn't look very butch."

"No," Kate said uncomfortably, "she doesn't."

"Has she asked you to marry her?"

"Be serious."

"To move in with you?"

"No."

"For money?"

Smiling, Kate shook her head. "She's brought food over, some plants, too. They really liven up the living room."

"Maybe she'd like to marry *me*," Maggie said. She leaned toward Kate. "Now that we've narrowed this down to your real concern, tell me what you think femme actually is."

"Not in control," Kate said tightly.

"Accepting your definition, which I don't, tell me — does Aimee have you running around in lace pinafores?"

Kate couldn't prevent a grin.

"Are you less butch on the job? Are you weeping over your corpses?"

"Not yet," Kate said, chuckling with nervous embarrassment, but relieved that the conversation was now exactly where she needed it to be.

"Are you deferring to your clumsy ox of a partner?"

"No. And Taylor's okay," she said.

"Patton claims she can still smell him in the floorboards of the Nightwood Bar."

"Taylor's okay," she repeated. "I could have a worse partner."

"How depressing," Maggie said. "Kate, do you have to be in control in every area of your life?"

"Don't you?"

"I've been in relationships where I've been femme."

Kate stared at Maggie's rugged-looking face and body. "Really," she said.

"Really." Maggie grinned at her. "The world's changed a lot since the sixties, Kate. Younger women have different ideas today. If you'd get around a little more —"

"I've been to bed with enough women," Kate retorted. "Maybe not legions, like you, but —"

"The first woman I was ever femme with was the one I was with the longest — two years. Sure I was surprised. Confused, too. Here I was a tough self-respecting butch, and Chrissie wanted to be the bow on my violin. But I tell you, Kate, after I'd spent so many days being a tiger on the streets, it was a relief to come home at night to be a pussycat in the sheets. I'm different ways with different partners now, sometimes my partner and I are different ways with each other. I like being all parts of a woman." She flung her Pall Mall into the fire. "You want to know what's really going on with you, Katie?"

Kate smiled faintly. "I'm listening, wise woman."

"Fools give you reasons, a wise woman wouldn't try. Tell me — whatever way she is with you, do you enjoy her?"

"Yes," she said. And added further: "Very much." Had she been willing to, she could not have conveyed the abandonment, the nirvana of the past ten nights.

"It's another part of you coming out. Another phase of your womanhood. That's all, Kate, nothing more. What are you getting her for Christmas?"

"Christmas? Kate gazed at her blankly, confused by this change of subject.

"Christmas." Maggie looked at the calendar on her watch. "Today's the thirteenth — eleven shopping days left."

"I'd better get busy," Kate said, getting up and coming over to where Maggie sat by the fire. She reached for Maggie's coffee mug. "Let me get you a refill." Then she leaned over, put her hands on Maggie's shoulders. "Thanks."

"She's lucky, you know," Maggie said teasingly, her coarse hands covering Kate's. "You're just now reaching your sexual peak. I'm sure she's enjoying you quite a lot."

As Kate walked toward the kitchen Maggie said, "Why don't you bring your gorgeous young lady to the bar some night?"

Kate turned at the doorway and grinned at her. "Why would I want to bring a woman who looks like Candice Bergen to the Nightwood Bar?"

— 20 —

After she left Maggie, Kate drove over Laurel Canyon into the city. A dim sense of necessity brought her to Arnaz Drive, and the Beverly Malibu. She parked her Nova across the street.

In unfiltered sunlight the beige stucco apartment building looked less garish than at night, an unadorned, shabby-genteel neighbor next to its taller, newer companions with their tasteful Christmas decorations. This area was zoned for four stories, and someday a developer would buy the Beverly Malibu and remodel or demolish it to add those two valuable extra levels.

Kate studied the building as if her laser-like concentration would act as a divining rod for its mysteries. Yesterday, toxicological testing of Sinclair's tissues had confirmed the presence of arsenic along with the fatal agent of strychnine. It was seventeen days ago that one of ten people in this building had attended a Thanksgiving Day party and had ended a man's life so savagely that the motive could only be vengeful hatred.

Kate took out her notebook and wrote the names of the partygoers, arranging them in ascending order of motive, pausing after each name, seeking for a countless time some element she might have overlooked. She did not write down Aimee's name.

Houston. No apparent motive, and plenty of troubles of his own.

Dorothy Brennan. The newest tenant, the woman with all the tragedy in her life. Her curiosity about Sinclair had triggered the argument at the party. Nothing in her background indicated any motive.

Paula Grant. A disdainful tolerance for the victim. Unlike other suspects, she, along with her dead lover, had suffered peripherally from the blacklist. The victim's incessant music was a motive — but only to a psychotic. And anyway, how could she seriously consider Paula?

Hazel Turner. Disliked the victim. His presence had disrupted her apartment building. Insufficient motive for murder, much less one this brutal.

Maxine Marlowe. Egotistic movie actress involved in a former romantic liaison with Sinclair. He'd taken what he wanted and then tossed her away. Possible deep-seated, festering rage over her sexual humiliation . . .

Parker Thomas. Contemptuous loathing for the victim, arising from profound ideological differences. A motive for wars throughout the history of the world, but was it an adequate motive for the murder of this one individual man?

Cyril Crane. Also had an ideological motive. Sinclair had informed on two gay acquaintances of his. But they were dead more than three decades.

She tapped her pen on Crane's name. Crane himself had an FBI file, closed in 1975 — the year that HUAC had been dissolved as a congressional committee. The non-political Cyril Crane had an FBI dossier because he had been known to them as a homosexual.

Even though no tenant of the Beverly Malibu was on the list of names Sinclair had given to HUAC, Taylor had run all the tenants' names through the FBI. Mildred A. Coates was cross-filed with known-Communist Andrew Coates. Paula Constance Grant had a dossier marked closed, as did Alice Rose Goldstein. Kate had suspected that Paula and Alice, as known associates of Paul Robeson, would have been the objects of FBI scrutiny during the McCarthy era, but the actuality of their names, along with Cyril Crane's, on a computer printout had incensed her, had roused both a personal and patriotic indignation that she could scarcely conceal from Taylor.

Kate turned to the list on the back page of her notebook. Taylor had checked further into FBI records of the eight people named by Sinclair, the names which Paula Grant had not been able to identify. John Robert Campbell and Randall Marlowe Reese had committed suicide, Campbell in 1954 and Reese in 1958. Alistair Todd Smythe had died in 1974. Of the remaining five, Martin Brooks Smythe and Gillian Jean Smythe had fled to England in 1952, but while their files were still open, they, along with Meaghan Dorothea Smythe, Robert Michael Tonelli, and Louise Brenda Tonelli, had not been under active surveillance since 1975.

Mildred Coates. Owen Sinclair as a stand-in for the informers who had destroyed her husband and ruined her own career? Very strong motive. But if Mildred Coates was emotionally capable of the crime, she seemed physically incapable of its execution. But Sinclair had been weakened by the poison administered at the party — and, Kate reflected, she had investigated a murder two years ago committed by a frail female killer . . .

Dudley Kincaid. Still the prime suspect. Taylor could not be persuaded to consider anyone else. Kincaid's screenplay had been stolen by Sinclair, plus, he blamed Sinclair for the writer's block which had only ended with Sinclair's death.

Kate ruminated over Dudley Kincaid, a man whose view of the world had hardened into moralizing patterns of black and white. Had he come to the psychotic belief that he would recover his talent only if Sinclair died in suitable expiation for the sin he had committed?

Kate sighed. Maybe — probably — Taylor was right that Kincaid was their man. But all the motive and probability in the world weren't enough to convict Kincaid or anyone else on her list of suspects. She and Taylor needed facts forming a tangible chain of evidence to the killer. And they had come up with virtually nothing.

She got out of the car, looked ruefully down at her clothes, then strode across the street to the Beverly Malibu, pulling her sweater down over her pants. With any luck Paula Grant would not see her.

Hazel buzzed Kate into the building and met her in the lobby. She reached to Kate, took her hand. "You're losing weight," she said reprovingly.

Smiling, Kate said, "I'm not on duty, Hazel. I was in the neighborhood and thought I'd stop in and tell you we're still on the case, we —"

"I've got beef stew," Hazel said, pulling Kate by the hand into her apartment. "Sit down, dear. I'll just whip up some lovely fluffy dumplings to go with it."

"Hazel, I appreciate it, but I just ate." The dark, furniture-stuffed living room was cozily warm. Kate inhaled appreciatively; the food odors were enticing. Apparently her appetite was returning. "How's it going here?"

"Terrible. You haven't arrested anybody, how else could it be but terrible?" With a shooing motion she dismissed Kate's attempt to explain. "I know you're doing your best. I'll get us some coffee and then I want to ask you something."

Making herself comfortable on the gold corduroy sofa, Kate looked at the small silver Christmas tree on the coffee table, and the four green urns forming a neat square around it. "Hello, Jerome," she greeted the urns, "how nice to see you all together."

Hazel's Persian cat sniffed a pant leg, then rubbed her face against the fabric of Kate's pants and purred. Kate leaned down. "Hello to you too, Precious." She stroked patterns in the soft white fur, thinking of Aimee's hair running like rivers of silk through her fingers.

Hazel, her voluminous orange housecoat floating out behind her, returned with a tray holding two mugs and a plate of chocolate-chip cookies. "First off," she said, "that apartment upstairs. I need it."

Kate took a mug of coffee and a cookie. "I realize that, Hazel. We can't unseal it just yet."

"Cyril came to me day before yesterday," Hazel said, sitting in the wing chair opposite Kate. "Jerome and me, we've been talking ever since. Cyril's with this group that's looking for places that don't cost an arm and a leg. For people with full-blown AIDS." She looked sternly at Kate. "I want to put two of 'em in that place upstairs. Jerome and me, we agree. What's going on about those people is a disgrace."

Surprised, Kate sipped her coffee and studied the landlady, wondering if Houston was one of the prospective tenants. She remembered Houston's remark about Hazel: "Anybody who thinks *The Diary of Anne Frank* is the best book ever written can't be all bad."

Hazel said, "If this thing hadn't happened to Owen, he'd still be living here, he'd still be paying me that little dab of rent, thanks to that rent control abomination." She scowled fiercely behind her steel-rimmed glasses. "Figuring all that, I'm not losing one cent if Cyril's people take the place for the same rent."

Kate suggested mildly, "You might risk losing

some of your tenants, Hazel. The ones who object to . . . their new neighbors."

"Lorraine Rothberg already told me she don't like it." Hazel picked up a package of Kents from the coffee table, shook out a cigarette. "I told her to go ahead and move, I'd use her apartment, too." She glared at Kate. "I told her I couldn't ever imagine somebody named *Rothberg* having the bird-brained gall to say such a thing."

Hazel lit the cigarette. "Do you suppose you can get Owen's place back to me by New Year's? It'd be nice to start out next year with somebody in there."

"I'll do my best," Kate promised. She gestured to the green urns. "Hazel, you and Jerome are really good people."

"Next question," Hazel said brusquely. Her voice suddenly softened: "Could you maybe find it in your heart to come over here for a time on Christmas Day?"

"Christmas Day?" Kate looked at her blankly. "Here?"

Hazel said, "Some of the tenants and me, we want to have another get-together. It don't look to us like you people are ever going to arrest anybody, and we can't have this cloud hanging over us. Even if everybody don't exactly like everybody else, even with all our quarreling, we used to be something like a family. I think my tenants would feel better about coming to another party if they knew somebody from the police was here." Her blue eyes were pleading. "Even for just a little time."

Kate was both touched and intrigued by the

request. "Who do you think would come to this party?"

"Same people as last time. Anybody who's got family is with them on holidays. The rest of us that are stuck here, we have a right to a little celebration without being scared about it."

Kate examined the idea. A detective, she quoted to herself, uses physical presence and insight as well as detection. And she and Taylor were getting nowhere with detection. Maybe watching the tenants together, interacting, would show her some new avenues. And there was an added bonus: Aimee had already spoken of her wish to spend a part of the day with Paula. Kate would have a legitimate excuse to be here as well. Another bonus: she could more easily extricate herself from Taylor's persistent invitations to come to his home for Christmas.

"I think it would be a good idea, Hazel," she said, and bit into a thick, moist chocolate-chip cookie.

The afternoon had darkened; a cold mist was blowing in from the Pacific. It really does feel like Christmas, Kate thought as she drove through festively decorated Beverly Hills. On a whim, she pulled onto Rodeo Drive.

This wealthiest of streets was jammed with people, most of them with cameras hung around their necks. The street was a panoply of miniature white lights, not only every store but every tree and every shrub a mass of sparkle magnified by reflections in shop windows. Small sculptured trees on the street's narrow median strip were decorated with red bows, the strip itself planted with poinsettias. Giorgio's every window and the trees alongside those windows were a shimmer of twinkle. At the end of Rodeo Drive stood the massive Beverly Wilshire Hotel outlined in lights.

In front of her, a red Jaguar convertible pulled away from the curb. A parking place on tiny Rodeo Drive during Christmas season? A miracle. Maybe an omen. Grinning, she pulled into the spot.

In the tall, elegant windows of Gucci she surveyed a display of small leather goods, most of them adorned by the interlocking GG of the Gucci insignia. GG — as in the two Grants. As in the two women entangled within her being . . .

Again she looked down at her clothing. Well, she seemed no more out of place than many other people on the street. Squaring her shoulders, she walked through the marble portals of Gucci.

The beige-carpeted store was crowded, filled with a quiet hum of commerce and the scents of expensive leather and perfume. She strolled amid clusters of customers, wondering if she could afford anything at all with those intertwined GGs. A sweatshirt on a standing rack attracted her. It was white, with a striking green abstract design on its front, and the GGs. She looked at the price: $195. "A *sweatshirt*," she muttered.

As she wandered into another room she noted security men everywhere, unobtrusive in their subdued suits, quietly watchful. She was drawn to a glass case containing ornamental key chains, most of them brilliant hues of red and green. There were also several with simply the intertwined GG in gold. One of those would be perfect. But was probably an astronomical price . . .

"May I help you?" inquired a woman from beside her.

Kate pointed. "How much is that one?"

"Thirty dollars."

Is that all, she started to say, and swallowed the words. "I'll take it."

The woman, brown-haired, in a green dress with a scarf at the throat, contemplated Kate. "Let us gift wrap it for you," she murmured, her direct gray eyes never leaving Kate's face.

"Thank you," Kate said.

"My pleasure indeed."

A few minutes later, a tiny Gucci shopping bag in hand, ridiculously pleased with herself, Kate got into her car. She would find something else for Aimee in the shops in Santa Monica. As she started up the Nova, she saw that a Volkswagen Rabbit had pulled into the parking place ahead of her. She laughed at its bumper sticker: DIE, TRENDY SCUM.

– 21 –

Kate entered the lobby of the Beverly Malibu at
2 p.m., as pre-arranged. "Merry Christmas," she
greeted Hazel, inhaling the aroma of roasting turkey;
it evoked happy Christmases of her past.

"Merry Christmas, darling," Hazel cooed, taking
her arm. "Now you just relax, everybody knows why
you're here. How very nice you look."

After much wavering, Kate had bought a pair of
gray crepe pants and a silk jacket, paisley-patterned
in gray and maroon tones. "It's wonderful on you,"
Aimee had murmured that morning, and added,

sensually stroking the jacket, "It feels like . . ." And left the sentence unfinished.

"Hazel, you look fine yourself," Kate said to the landlady, who wore a floor-length pink chemise adorned with white and yellow flowers.

Kate peered into the community room. Paula, standing beside a counter which held a large punch bowl, was talking with Aimee and also Parker Thomas, who appeared more elfin than Kate remembered in his neatly trimmed beard and his bright red V-neck sweater over a white shirt and plaid tie.

Kate's gaze lingered on Paula. Trim and elegant in a black jacket and a long, deep green skirt, she was speaking now to Parker Thomas, gesturing with one hand which held a cigarette, the other hand, pale and slim, resting on his arm. Kate noticed Aimee looking at her, and she quickly smiled, guilty with her pleasure in Paula. Especially after this morning . . . and especially when Aimee herself looked so beautiful, her thick dark hair glossy against her cream-colored blouse. Both women, she thought, both women are so . . .

She pulled her gaze away to appraise the room. It was imperative that she concentrate.

At the long table sat Mildred Coates in a black dress and pearls, and Dorothy Brennan, only slightly less somber in a gray top over a navy blue skirt. They were listening with obvious enjoyment to Cyril Crane, who lounged in careless ease between them, freshly barbered, suavely handsome, every inch the movie star in his gold brocade shirt and tan trousers. Houston, Kate knew, was spending a few weeks with friends in Santa Barbara. Maxine Marlowe had not as yet appeared, nor had Dudley Kincaid. They would turn up; Hazel had guaranteed it.

Kate entered the room with calculated casualness. "Merry Christmas, everyone."

She was answered by a chorus of similar greetings. Cyril Crane rose, shook her hand, as did Parker Thomas, who sent puffs from his meerschaum pipe into the reek of cigarette smoke in the room. Dorothy Brennan took Kate's hand and held it between her two. "So very delightful you're here," she said in her slightly clipped tones.

Kate smiled, responding to the warm embrace of Dorothy's hands and her words. But what about Paula? Aimee had more than once said Paula approved of their relationship, but as Paula approached, Kate suddenly felt an odd sense of culpability, an edgy apprehension.

"It's good to see you again, Detective Delafield," Paula said formally.

Kate barely registered the cool hand briefly in hers. The perceptive hazel eyes were unreadable. "The pleasure is mine," Kate murmured.

"Have some punch," Aimee said, offering a glass cup filled with burgundy-colored liquid.

"Alcohol?" Kate asked quietly, accepting the cup.

"Not so you'd notice."

The eyes meeting hers were so dark with intimacy that Kate, with Paula looking at her, felt exposed like an X-ray. She and Aimee had been together in public in restaurants, but not with anyone who knew them.

Early this morning Kate had opened and donned her gift from Aimee — a luxurious white robe monogrammed with her initials. Aimee had unwrapped the vivid blue jacket-sweater Kate had found for her, then the package with the Gucci key ring. Kate had attached to it a key to her apartment. The lovemaking afterward, Aimee's lengthy and consuming possession of her, was still palpable between them.

"Come try my vegetable dip," Hazel said, taking Kate's arm. Kate allowed herself to be led away. She could not be distracted by Aimee, nor could she concern herself with Paula. Hazel said, "You just help yourself to everything, darling. I'll bring in our lovely turkey."

Taking her time over the relish tray and several dishes of unshelled nuts, Kate observed the room. The four urns rested on top of the television behind a row of green Christmas lights; the TV, its sound turned off, was tuned to *Miracle on 34th Street.* Sipping cranberry-flavored punch, Kate listened to the tenants' conversation — the cold and cloudy weather, the Armenian earthquake, the explosion over Scotland of Pam Am Flight 103.

"Let's pack up this whole goddam show and take it on the road," crowed Maxine Marlowe from the doorway. Arm-in-arm with Dudley Kincaid, the actress swept into the room, her off-the-shoulder red taffeta dress in rustling accompaniment. She sailed directly over to Kate, adding her cloying perfume to the room's smoke. "Our protector," she said with a mocking salute. The odor of gin reached Kate; Maxine had obviously fortified herself for the rigors of this party.

Her bright red mouth grinning widely in her garish face, Maxine extended a hand, its middle finger covered to the knuckle by an enormous emerald ring. Warily, Kate reached out; Maxine's fingertips lightly

220

tapped hers and withdrew. Then Maxine slid her arm from Dudley Kincaid and moved away, chuckling.

He stared coldly at Kate through his steel-rimmed trifocals. "This being Christmas," he said, "I trust you left your handcuffs at home."

She looked back at him, at the sprinkling of dandruff on the shoulders of his dark brown jacket. "I brought red and green ones," she said.

From her right she heard a chuckle from Aimee, a guffaw from Maxine Marlowe. "You stay right beside her, Dudley dear," Maxine called. "Remember what happened to the last man I escorted in here."

Dorothy Brennan rose from the table, came over to help herself to olives from the relish tray. "Merry Christmas, Mr. Kincaid. Do taste this lovely punch. How's your screenplay coming along?"

"I've finished the first segment and it's solid," he said, beaming at her as he took his Camels and a box of matches from a jacket pocket. "Thank you for asking."

"Can you tell us what it's about? Or do you not talk about your work?"

Kate heard a sigh of exasperation; somehow she knew it came from Paula.

Kincaid scraped fire onto a match-head. "It correlates Hollywood today with the fifties." He lit his Camel. "And the corruption — worse than anything we'd even begun to fear back then. My major character is a principled moral hero —"

"Ah yes, the moral hero," said Parker Thomas, leaning back against the counter, puffing from his pipe. "One must always have a moral hero battling against all odds — to justify his unconscionable deeds."

221

If Dorothy Brennan had meant to tactfully defuse the confrontation between herself and Kincaid, Kate thought, she'd just tossed a match onto gasoline.

"Some of us," Dudley Kincaid said acidly, "do try to live our lives in accordance with a higher morality."

Cyril Crane said, tilting back on his chair, "Some of us feel that the higher morality is the first amendment to the Constitution."

"Oh fucking shit," Maxine said. She plunged a carrot stick into dip and crunched it as if wishing it were someone's bones.

Kincaid said to Crane, "People like you always hide behind the first amendment. You and your card-carrying friends at the ACLU exploit democratic freedoms in order to undermine them. You —"

"People like you," Parker Thomas said, "believe patriotism means marching in step behind the thought police."

"Left wing *hogwash*." Kincaid turned his back and ladled himself some punch.

"I seem to have done it again," Dorothy muttered to no one in particular as Kincaid sipped from his cup and then carried it back to the table.

"You knew what his play's about — I told you." Mildred Coates' voice quavered with anger.

"I was being polite," Dorothy said, throwing her hands up. "Trying to make peace . . ."

"— the words of Adolf Hitler, the immortal Oliver North, and Dudley Kincaid," Parker Thomas was saying, "patriotic love of country justifies anything."

"Everyone, come here," Hazel said severely. She had entered the room bearing a platter with a steaming, golden brown turkey. She lowered the platter to the table. "Just *look* at this gorgeous bird. It's *Christmas*. Quit this political palaver, we're all just plain sick to death of it. Somebody get busy and carve." She marched toward the door. "I'll be right back with the trimmings."

"I'll help," Aimee said, and followed her.

"Hazel's right," Paula said emphatically, her arms crossed.

Kincaid was staring at Parker Thomas, his moustache bristling over lips tight with anger. "How dare you compare Colonel North and me to Adolf Hitler."

Thomas, his pale green eyes fixed on Kincaid, shrugged. "Maybe it's your Hitler moustache, Dudley."

Maxine Marlowe picked up the carving knife. "Here," she said, handing the implement to Dorothy Brennan. "You're the only one I trust with a knife." Her laughter rang harshly in the room.

Obediently, Dorothy Brennan began to carve, sawing easily through a leg joint and beginning on the breast meat. "Dear," she said to Mildred Coates, who was staring at Dudley Kincaid with a hand at her throat, "please come help us dish up."

Mildred shook her head. She removed her glasses with their built-in hearing aid, placed them gently on the table. Her face was pinched with pain.

"Here you are, my man," Maxine said, forking some white meat onto a plate and handing it to Kincaid. "Nice tender breast. I bet you haven't had any for months. Maybe years."

He took the plate and clapped it down on the table. "When it comes to preserving this country, a real American understands patriotism. You —" He jabbed a finger at Thomas, "you'd betray this country out of your misguided, simple-minded —"

"*You're* simple-minded," Cyril Crane snapped. "When was the last time an American sold out this country for any reason except money?"

"Here, honey," Maxine Marlowe said, handing Cyril Crane a plate of sliced turkey, "stick this in your mouth and chew real slow."

Crane smiled suddenly, charmingly. He accepted the plate and sat down at the table. "Thank you, Maxine darling."

"Everybody, please," Hazel pleaded as she and Aimee came back into the room carrying trays. "Here's nice dressing and gravy and cranberry sauce, candied sweet potatoes and rolls, fresh nice peas and jello salad. Let's eat up and forget all this foolish —"

"We only know about the enemies we see," Kincaid said gratingly. "We tried to clean out this town once — now we've got creatures like Norman Lear and Fonda and Hayden crawling out of the woodwork, we've got —"

"Lucille Ball," Cyril Crane said around a mouthful of turkey.

"*Lucille Ball?*" Aimee laughed as if at an absurdity.

"A dupe," Kincaid said in dismissal.

"A registered member of the Communist Party," Thomas said cheerfully, knocking the contents of his pipe into an ashtray. "I'll take a drumstick," he said to Dorothy Brennan.

"I thought you'd read all the history, dear," Paula said to Aimee. "She joined the Party when she was young, like most people who did. They tried to hush it up, it leaked out and HUAC cleared her. Other people's lives were ruined over far, far less, but she was America's darling. Call it a triumph of celebrity over politics."

"All HUAC ever did was destroy lives," Cyril Crane stated. "They never accomplished one damn thing beyond that."

"Left wing revisionist history," Kincaid sneered. "We'd only begun to get the job done. Joe McCarthy was broken by a left wing conspiracy."

Kate heard the rustle of taffeta as Maxine came up beside her. "Sweetheart, you couldn't see your way to lending me your gun, could you?"

"Hopeless ignoramuses." Kincaid sat down at the table and dispiritedly pulled his plate of turkey toward him. "I don't know why I even bother."

"Neither do we," Paula said. "You won't change the viewpoint of a single person in this room. Isn't that right, Detective Delafield?"

Kate started at Paula's mention of her name, but recovered quickly and smiled; she could hardly introduce her own opinion that Kincaid was a priggish, arrogant bigot. She said lightly, "News people and police aren't entitled to a viewpoint."

There were a few relieved chuckles; the atmosphere in the room seemed to change. Mildred Coates picked up her glasses and put them on. Hazel said, "That's more like it. Now let's all eat hearty."

Kate, with Aimee beside her, joined the tenants who stood at the table. "To peace," Dorothy Brennan said quietly, and raised her cup. "However we find it."

"To peace," Kate echoed along with everyone else, and drank from her cup of punch.

There was a sound from Dudley Kincaid; he

lurched sideways, spilling his glass of punch across the paper tablecloth. Jabbing a finger at the spilled punch he tried to speak, staggered, doubled over.

"Oh God is this some kind of joke?" Aimee's voice trembled.

Kate stood in stupefaction as Kincaid, gagging, a hand clawing at his throat, collapsed to his knees. He groped toward her.

Galvanized into action, shouldering Cyril Crane aside, she ran to him, and knelt and gripped his shoulders. Again he tried to speak, his head jerking, his glasses falling to the floor. Perspiration beaded his face.

"Paula, call nine-one-one," she commanded. "Get the paramedics."

She heard running footsteps, cries of consternation from around her as she circled Kincaid's shoulders and lowered him to the floor. He was gasping; and his breath smelled distinctly of bitter almonds. In despair she loosened his tie and unbuttoned his shirt, feeling for the pulse in his throat. It was rapid, but faint.

"You'll be okay," she encouraged him.

But his appalled, gaping eyes told her that he knew the truth. His gasping ceased, his body became violently spastic, his heels beating a tattoo on the floor. Finally his body stilled. His blue gaze became fixed and unseeing.

"God, oh God," she heard Aimee sob.

"Aimee, I need backup. Tell Paula," she ordered.

She had failed. She had come here as a police officer at Hazel Turner's request, and failed. Now she could do nothing more than preserve this scene of death and seek a double murderer. Her futility forming into a white ball of rage, she looked up.

Hazel had backed up against the television set; the four green urns were clasped tightly to her chest. Parker Thomas was bent over the counter, his face buried in his arms, Maxine Marlowe's hand on his back; she stared at Kate, her face ashen in spite of her makeup. Cyril Crane, an arm supporting Mildred Coates, was half-leading, half-carrying her from the room.

Kate's gaze froze on Dorothy Brennan. Her dark eyes, riveted on Dudley Kincaid, were wide and glittering as if in fever. Her lips were drawn back over her teeth, her broad face was a feral mask.

"Maxine." Kate used the actress's first name to add authority to her words. "Help me. Hazel, I need your apartment. I need to get everyone in there, and fast. I'm counting on you both not to let anyone talk to anyone else."

"You got it, sister." Maxine gripped Parker Thomas and Dorothy Brennan by the arm. Dorothy stumbled and caught her balance as Maxine pulled her toward the doorway. The glittering eyes were still fixed on Dudley Kincaid.

Hazel moved toward the door, cradling her urns, her face wet with tears. Her gravelly voice was a whisper: "You've got to find out who's doing this."

"Yes, Hazel," Kate answered. "I know."

– 22 –

Taylor arrived an hour later, his face a baleful contradiction to the festive plaid of his new Christmas jacket.

Kate had recovered her composure; she understood that no power of hers could have saved Dudley Kincaid. "Merry Christmas," she offered wryly.

"Yeah, sure." He hunkered down beside Kincaid's staring corpse, and peered up at her. "Suicide, right?"

"Wrong."

"Shit." He heaved a sigh. "So now we got seven

suspects. So we wait through six more holidays, arrest whoever's left."

Dutifully, she smiled. Heaving another sigh, he stood up and yanked out his notebook.

She sat at the far end of the table with him, away from Kincaid's body, and without referring to the copious notes she had made while patrol officers secured the building, she related every detail she could remember of the party, every scrap of conversation, all the particulars of Kincaid's death, patiently waiting as Taylor recorded her eyewitness account, hoping he might ask some question that would elicit a memory that had eluded her consciousness. She purposefully delayed reporting her observations of Dorothy Brennan.

Pointing under the table to a plastic vial circled in chalk, she said, "The cyanide was in that."

"Cyanide?"

"I'm assuming. His breath smelled like almonds, he was dead in less than a minute. The tenants are in Hazel's apartment. I advised all them of their Miranda rights, had them empty their pockets. Mildred Coates was the only one with a purse — she permitted a search. Hansen and I did pat downs —"

Even to Aimee and Paula. Aimee, who had submitted in frozen compliance.

"We didn't find a thing. Which isn't surprising. When Sinclair died we didn't find a container for the strychnine. This time she knew better than to risk having a container found on her, or using a capsule that would leave traces on her hands."

"She? Her?"

She braced herself. "Ed, as sure we're both sitting

here, Dorothy Brennan killed Owen Sinclair and Dudley Kincaid."

He gaped at her. *"Why?"*

She had little choice but to confess, "I have no idea. She could simply be insane — psychotic."

He looked down at his notebook, pushing his fleshy lips in and out. She could not blame him for his incredulity. In their initial and follow-up interviews with Dorothy Brennan she had seemed a woman of convincing calm, of motherly warmth and sensibility.

"I've got no proof," she admitted. "But I'm certain she did it."

"So tell me what you've got."

Convince me, he was saying. She opened her notebook. "Dorothy Brennan knew better than to give Kincaid any of the punch —" Unlike Aimee, who had lovingly offered it to her. Aimee . . . who was safely, securely with Paula until Kate was finished here and could come to her . . . "— but she urged him to taste it." She gestured to the punch bowl behind them. "It's cranberry-flavored, perfect for disguising the taste of a powerful poison — just like Sinclair's bourbon disguised the strychnine. She knew what Kincaid's screenplay was about but she asked anyway, knowing it was sure-fire to start an argument, create a diversion. Just like when she killed Sinclair. Sinclair was drinking bourbon, she had no problem administering the poison. But she couldn't be sure Kincaid would drink his punch, so she made sure by proposing a toast. When Kincaid collapsed, she discarded the container. We'll laser print it, but we know from Sinclair's apartment that she's too smart to leave prints." She paused, searching for response in his face.

"So far I'm with you."

"Ed, all the shops we canvassed about the opera album and handcuffs — we got nowhere because Brennan's only lived in the Beverly Malibu nine months, not long enough to be in any of the photos Hazel loaned us."

He nodded. "Possible."

She warmed to her argument. "She stole his keys at his Fourth of July party. Periodically she came into his apartment to spike his bourbon with arsenic, and she knew when to do it. Paula told us Sinclair never left his apartment without slamming the door off the hinges, and Hazel told us Brennan was always out snooping around the building."

Taylor's eyes were half-closed, his pen tapping on his notebook.

"Sinclair came upstairs after the party, stripped down to his shorts and went to bed. If he was sick enough to call for help, his phone cord was cut, she'd done that beforehand — she arrived at the party after Sinclair.

"Then she came into his apartment. She's a big woman, capable of holding him down and attaching a handcuff to his wrist and then the headboard. And she had the advantage of surprise. That chair beside Sinclair's bed — we know someone sat there to watch him die. We found no ashtrays in the room. All our suspects smoke — except for Hazel, who hardly counts as a smoker, and Dorothy Brennan."

"Kate . . ." He shifted in his chair. "What you're saying is well and good but it's —"

"Conjecture." She took a deep breath and plunged ahead. "After Kincaid died, I looked at her. Ed, she was like an animal standing over its kill. *Gloating* over its kill. *Gorging* itself on its kill. She was like a . . ." She groped for more words.

"Kate, is this one of those woman's intuition things?"

She sagged in her chair.

He scratched his bald spot. "Let's say I'm Dorothy Brennan's lawyer."

"Ed, I told you I had no proof," she said through gritted teeth.

"Yeah, but I'm not talking proof." Taylor pointed to the plastic vial. "Look how close it is to him. Brennan's lawyer would say Dudley used it on himself, dropped it."

"Ed." She tried to control her burgeoning anger, her sense of betrayal by her own partner. "He didn't kill himself. I was here. I saw him die. The man died in my arms."

"Yeah, and that's rough, Kate. I was thinking about that on the way over here." Taylor's brown eyes, soft with sympathy, left her face to survey Kincaid's body. "Stiffs I've seen by the umpteen, but always after the fact."

He was responding to the emotional content in her words, not the logic. Kate argued, "He gave no hint of suicide in anything he said or did. There was no indication whatever."

"Kate," he said with an odd gentleness, "think about the suicides we've handled where the family said the same thing. Kincaid was weird — you got to admit that. What you saw maybe isn't what you think you saw."

Fury overcame her ability to speak. Looking into her face he said, "Ease up, partner." He held out his hands placatingly. "Your theory's gonna fly with the D.A.? We'll get an arrest warrant based on what you saw in Dorothy Brennan's face?"

"Of course not," she muttered.

"Well, okay, let's just keep an open mind to every angle. Let's talk to people, get some supporting statements."

She nodded concession. "We'll start with Paula Grant." And Aimee. That way she could release the two of them to take care of each other. "Leave Dorothy Brennan for last. You ask all the questions so I don't lead or influence anyone with my own observations. Let's find out what everybody else saw."

He sighed. "Guess we'll need to take everybody to the station this time."

She had already dismissed the prospect. There was no point in subjecting the tenants of the Beverly Malibu — other than Dorothy Brennan — to further ordeal. "Let's set up chairs in the laundry room downstairs, use it as an interview room."

"Sure, good idea. Real nice jacket," he said, a peace offering.

She accepted the offering. "Yours is very snazzy."

"You look really good these days, Kate," he said. "What's going on with you?"

Momentarily, she juggled the question. "A new exercise program," she said.

"Aimee's lying down," Paula said, a hand on Kate's arm, her gaze intent and apologetic, her tone impersonal — for Taylor's benefit, Kate knew. "Please wait till tomorrow to talk to her. Hazel's given her something to calm her — I do think it's best she stay here tonight."

"Of course," Kate said perfunctorily, feeling desolate. Aimee would remain here because she preferred to. She wanted no contact with Kate, with this direct and continuing involvement in catastrophe and fatality. *To her I'm Dr. Death.*

"Aimee's so young," Paula said softly, still for Kate's comfort. "A benefit of age is that we understand how tenuous life really is. At least this business with Owen and Dudley is all over now."

"All over, Paula?" Taylor queried. Kate looked at her in dismay.

"Well . . . yes. It is, isn't it?" She seated herself in one of the card table chairs Hazel had provided. "You did arrest Dudley —"

"No ma'am, we took him in for questioning. There wasn't enough evidence to arrest him."

"Whatever. The truth is, he did kill Owen, didn't he? We all know about the stolen screenplay. And now he's killed himself. He did kill himself, didn't he?"

Taylor did not look at Kate. "For the time being we have to treat it as a suspicious death."

"Of course. It's why we had to be searched. We all understood that."

Paula answered Taylor's questions briefly, tiredly, her face pale against the white walls of the small room. She added no new detail to Kate's observations of the party.

"After Mr. Kincaid collapsed," Taylor said, "did you notice anything strange about any other tenant, any strange behavior?"

"Other than being horrified? What else would there be?"

Taylor asked, "Does it seem weird to you that he'd kill himself?"

"Weird?" She repeated the word with distaste. "The man was a bitter eccentric, an intellectual fossil." She gestured to Kate. "As your own partner can confirm from the conversation at the party today."

Kate and Taylor next called for Mildred Coates. "It's all been so awful," she quavered tearfully in the doorway of the room, "I'm so terribly upset." They took a brief statement that she had not witnessed anything unusual, and released her.

Parker Thomas slumped over on his card table chair, ceaselessly rubbing his fingers through his beard. "It's his ghastly form of retribution," he uttered, closing his eyes. "I'm sure he died believing he'd avenged every injury, real or imagined, he'd ever received from anyone in the Beverly Malibu." Like Paula Grant he was bewildered by the question about unusual behavior from any other tenant.

As was Cyril Crane, who expressed certainty that Kincaid had taken revenge on Sinclair, then used the Christmas party "to inject his miserable self permanently into the unwilling memories of every single one of us at the Beverly Malibu."

Maxine Marlowe sat with her plump knees crossed, twisting her emerald ring around and around on her finger. Her voice echoed in the tiled room, harsh and so slurred that Kate suspected that Hazel had given Maxine a calming potion along with Aimee. "Dudley the dud. He could never get it up his whole damn life. Dudley the dud had to use poison on himself — he couldn't even point a gun, much less you know what."

Hazel Turner, Kate's final hope, said to Kate, "At first, you know, at first I thought somebody'd done him in just like Owen. But now that I've thought on it, I see Dorothy's right."

"Dorothy?" chimed Kate and Taylor.

"Well . . . yes. She's been telling all of us that Dudley did it to himself, and of course she's right, and it's a comfort knowing so. Dorothy's a fine woman."

As Hansen escorted Hazel away, Kate said to Taylor, "So much for uncontaminated eyewitness testimony."

"Yeah," he said sourly. "Let's interrogate the bitch."

"I'd like to see her apartment again," Kate said. "Let's take her there to talk to her."

But the lab team had arrived, and also Lieutenant Bodwin, who conferred with Kate and Taylor before dealing with the reporters, a small contingent on this Christmas Day evening. To assist in establishing official cause of death, Bodwin suggested, the coroner's office should also look into this second, but more ambiguous, death at the Beverly Malibu.

"Yes, sir," Kate said evenly.

* * * * *

236

Dorothy Brennan preceded Kate and Taylor into her living room with slow, heavy steps. "May I offer you tea? Coffee?"

"Not a thing, ma'am," Taylor answered as he and Kate sat on the sofa. Dorothy Brennan settled into the Danish-modern armchair.

Kate glanced swiftly around. The room seemed different. The comfortable clutter, present during their two earlier interviews, was gone; there were no magazines or papers scattered about, and the ever-present plastic-swathed library books had been stacked neatly on the gray formica desk. The table which had held the disarray of Brennan's family photos was now empty.

Taylor had also noticed. "The pictures," he said, gesturing to the table.

"Christmas is not a good day to look at pictures of my children."

"Yes, ma'am, sorry."

Kate crossed her arms. Dorothy Brennan had already put Taylor at a psychological disadvantage. Taylor said in a subdued voice, "Would you tell us what you saw at the party today."

In tones as hushed and reverential as if she were in a church, Dorothy Brennan related the events of the party in the same complete detail that Kate had given Taylor, again berating herself for beginning the argument involving Kincaid. "But," she concluded, "nothing I did made any difference. He killed himself, I saw it."

Kate stared at her. Taylor said, "You did?"

Dorothy Brennan intercepted Kate's stare. The dark brown eyes held hers, scoured hers in cold, brilliant perception, like a searchlight in a prison yard.

The eyes shifted away, releasing Kate from their icy vise. *This woman is a monster.* The knowledge sank into the marrow of Kate's bones.

Then Dorothy Brennan said quietly, her face neutral, "I saw him drop a container onto the floor just as he drank his punch."

Composing herself with considerable effort, Kate framed her question carefully: "Do you know if anyone else saw the same thing?"

Dorothy Brennan looked at her, the brown eyes shuttered. "Did you?"

"My partner's not at liberty to say," Taylor answered. "Would you answer her question?"

"I don't really know," Dorothy Brennan replied. "We were drinking a toast. I simply happened to be looking at him at the time."

Of course you were. Kate studied her. The face was peaceful, slightly flushed. The face contained gratification, as if after thoroughly satisfying sex.

Taylor said, "When my partner gathered all of you in Hazel Turner's apartment, she ordered you not to talk to each other. Why did you tell everybody Mr. Kincaid killed himself?"

"Because he had. It was my duty to say something because everyone was petrified that we had another murder on our hands."

Nodding, Taylor wrote in his notebook. Then he led her through a series of questions about her acquaintance with Dudley Kincaid. Finally he turned to Kate. "Any more questions?"

"Not at this moment," she answered, her gaze fixed on Dorothy Brennan's face. The brown eyes met hers again. They were tranquil, untroubled.

Kate stalked out of the building, Taylor following. She turned on him. "Did you see her look at me? Did you?"

"When? What do you mean?" His face was a picture of confusion.

She wanted to pound on him. "She did it, Ed. As sure as the sun will rise tomorrow, she did it. Did you listen to all that detail of the party? She saw as much as I did. Did you hear that voice describing everything? She's a killer who loves to kill. She watches and memorizes every second of when she kills."

"Partner," he said softly, nodding, "your say-so is good enough for me. But this isn't *Murder, She Wrote*. We can't do a thing without proof, we can't take her in without PC."

Probable cause. The evening chill penetrating her silk jacket, Kate stood in white-knuckled frustration. Probable cause. Her certainty, even as primary investigating officer, that this woman had committed two vicious homicides for pleasure, meant nothing. What she had seen on Dorothy Brennan's face and in her eyes, the theory she had constructed about the commission of the crimes, did not constitute probable cause. And probable cause, the handcuffs the courts put on the police, must dictate every step she took or even the strongest case would land on the list of prosecutions dismissed for procedural error.

"You think I'm wrong, don't you, Ed," she said quietly.

"No. I believe you because you believe it. It's just hard for me to see the woman doing it."

"I'm right, Ed. And unless we can find grounds to arrest this woman, other people in the Beverly Malibu are going to die."

– 23 –

Kate entered her apartment in the early hours of the morning, her depression deepened by awareness that her bedroom would be empty for the first time in the twenty-two days since Aimee had come to her.

But the room was not empty. In surging joy she sat down on the edge of the bed as Aimee rolled over and focused slumberous eyes on her. Kate leaned down, kissed her forehead. "I'm so glad you're here," she said simply.

"I had to try out my new key," Aimee murmured,

cupping Kate's face in sleep-warmed hands. "What's . . . is everything okay?"

"We're . . . still working. I've only got a few hours, I need to get back." She would not tell Aimee about Dorothy Brennan as yet. But she would make Aimee absolutely safe from her, whatever she had to do. Aimee and Paula. "Everything is okay, I promise," she said.

Aimee rolled back into her sleeping position. "Come in with me, I'll hold you."

After she showered, Kate lay for the next hour cradled but not soothed by Aimee's warmth. At five o'clock, to drowsy moans of protest, Kate gently disentangled herself and got up. Wearing the robe Aimee had given her for Christmas, she took a mug of coffee into the living room.

She sat in an armchair and pored over her notebooks of the Sinclair and Kincaid deaths, marshaling her concentration, reviewing facts, examining every note about Dorothy Brennan.

Brennan was sixty-three, had held a series of mundane jobs, had lived with her husband's mother since the husband's death fourteen years ago. One daughter had shot herself at a very early age; a son had been lost to drugs; the other daughter had sequestered herself in England.

The Brennan children. Yesterday their photos had been missing from the table in Brennan's apartment . . . Kate ransacked her memory, trying to visualize the assortment of family photos she had looked at during the first interview with Dorothy Brennan. No, she decided. In none of those photos had the father of those children appeared — Dorothy Brennan's husband.

The husband. *My husband's family is English,* Dorothy Brennan had said. Brennan had lived with her husband's English mother . . . A daughter had gone to England. England . . .

She turned to the back of her notebook and the list of names Sinclair had given to the House Committee on Un-American Activities:

John Robert Campbell
Randall Marlowe Reese
Alistair Todd Smythe
Gillian Anne Smythe
Martin Brooks Smythe
Meaghan Dorothea Smythe
Robert Michael Tonelli
Louise Brenda Tonelli

"Dorothy Brennan. *Brennan,*" she whispered into the silence of the living room. She said aloud, "Kate Delafield, you're a fool."

She went into her bedroom. Quickly, quietly, she dressed. Then wrote a note to Aimee that she would call as soon as she possibly could. Thirty-five minutes later she pulled into the parking lot at Wilshire Division.

Two hours later, confirmation came in by teletype. From the elimination prints taken of the tenants in the Beverly Malibu and faxed to the FBI, Dorothy Brennan's prints had come up positive. Dorothy Brennan was Meaghan Dorothea Smythe, wife of

Alistair Smythe; she and her husband had been among those named to the House Un-American Activities Committee by Owen Charles Sinclair.

"I still don't get it," Taylor complained as he climbed into the Plymouth for the drive to the Beverly Malibu. "Okay, she went bonkers and got back at Sinclair the worst way she could dream up. But why in hell did she kill Dudley?"

"Possibly she wanted to plant the idea of his suicide to cover her murder of Sinclair. But I doubt it. If the woman is lethally clever, she's also lethally insane. My guess is, she killed him because he was a right-winger who defended Sinclair's informing. Maybe because I was there she elected to kill him quickly instead of torturing him like Sinclair."

"Jesus," Taylor muttered, "I'm glad I didn't mention I vote Republican."

She grinned at him and started the Plymouth. Soon they would have this psychotic killer in handcuffs and out of the Beverly Malibu. "Paula Grant told me Alistair Smythe was an actor. Dorothy Brennan didn't have a photo of him on that table because she couldn't risk having anyone recognize him."

"That's another thing, Kate. Why wouldn't Sinclair recognize Dorothy Brennan?"

"That puzzles me too, Ed," she admitted. "From the photo the FBI faxed to us, she hasn't changed all that much over the years. But then, she's so ordinary-looking a woman . . ."

"That smashed picture frame with the missing photo of McCarthy —"

"She probably defaced it," Kate said.

"Yeah. Maybe used it for toilet paper. The name business was right there all the time," Taylor growled, slapping aside the straps of his seatbelt and crossing his arms in disgust. "My dumb mistake."

"*My* dumb mistake," Kate corrected him as she pulled onto Venice Boulevard, two backup black-and-whites behind her. "I assumed Brennan retained her husband's name after his death. I've been a cop too long to ever assume. But Brennan made a major mistake by telling us her husband's family was English, and we should've caught it. How could her name be Brennan if her husband had two English parents?"

"Yeah, and I blew that part bad, Kate," Taylor said. "Me with an Irish mother, me growing up on Walter Brennan movies."

"You? Delafield is an English name. I'm the one who should've known Brennan is Irish."

Dorothy Brennan had vanished from the Beverly Malibu.

"How should I know when she left," Hazel said in testy response to their eager questioning. "And what are all these police for? The neighbors must think the Beverly Malibu is worse than Iran. I got up at six like I usually do and there was this envelope hanging on my door, this note in it and two hundred-dollar bills."

Kate studied the note:

My dear Hazel,
I must move on now. Urgent business awaits
me. Please return my library books and call
Enterprise Rents to pick up their furniture.
Anything else can be given or thrown away. I
hope the enclosed will help compensate for your
trouble. Dear, good-hearted Hazel, I wish you
health and long life, as I do everyone at the
Beverly Malibu.

Dorothy Brennan

Taylor said to Hazel, "You knew she rented her furniture?"

"Sonny, like I told you before, I know everything that goes on in my building."

"You didn't think that was weird enough to tell us?"

"You're saying it's weirder than anything else my tenants do? Besides, Dorothy wouldn't harm a fly."

"We'll need to look over her apartment, Hazel," Kate told her. *Urgent business awaits me,* the note had said. When they had last talked to Dorothy Brennan the apartment had been neat. The library books stacked, no pictures of her children . . . She had been packed to leave before she killed Dudley Kincaid. They had to find this woman, and fast.

Hazel clutched Kate's arm. "Honey, you sealed up Owen's place. Then Dudley's place and the community room. Now Dorothy's place. Rent control's better than you police."

Kate patted her hand. "Don't worry, Hazel — we'll soon be releasing all your property back to you."

* * * * *

Shortly after the APB was issued for Meaghan Dorothea Smythe, aka Dorothy Brennan, suspicion of two counts of homicide, possibly armed, considered extremely dangerous, her 1982 beige Honda Civic was located at a used car lot on La Brea, sold for cash on December 22 of the previous week.

In her apartment the photos of her children were gone, but apparently little else — not even basic articles of clothing or toiletries. "Looks like she walked outta here with just her purse," Taylor muttered as he and Kate searched abandoned rooms that held the sterile air of a motel. "And maybe her bag of poisons," Kate suggested. Pending toxicological evaluation of a few over-the-counter medications and some foodstuffs, they had found no evidence of toxic agents.

"We've got her previous address in Silverlake," she said. "Let's go check it out."

– 24 –

Kate and Taylor parked on Hyperion, in front of numerals written in large white script on a gray fence overburdened with shrubbery. A latched gate led to stairs cemented into a grassy, sunlit hill, then to a stucco ranch-style house overlooking a portion of Silverlake and the hazy tops of downtown buildings.

A slender white-haired woman, clad in earth-stained brown corduroys and a heavy cotton work shirt rolled to the elbows, knelt in one of four large flower beds fronting the house, energetically weeding. Glimpsing Kate and Taylor, she sat back on her heels and removed her gardening gloves, then climbed to her feet with effort, the gloves hanging from one hand, the weeding tool from the other.

Kate extended identification, as did Taylor. "I'm Detective Delafield, this is Detective Taylor, Los Angeles Police Department."

The woman stiffened; her pale blue eyes scanned Kate, then fastened on Taylor in open hostility. "Now what? What do you want?"

Kate asked courteously, "May we know your identity?"

"What is it you want?" The tone was glacial.

"We're investigating a double homicide," Kate replied. "We have information that the person we believe is responsible lived here for a number of years."

The woman tossed her weeding tool aside; it thudded into soft, well-cultivated earth. Slowly slapping her gardening gloves against a thigh, she stared into their faces. Kate waited, studying the aged face with its pale skin almost transparent over the long thin nose, the withered flesh below sharply defined cheekbones, the small mouth with a refinement enhanced rather than diminished by the years. The entire face was filled with a tense vitality. "A true believer's face," Kate's father would have described it.

"I'll talk to you," the woman said, motioning to Kate.

"We —"

"You or no one."

This peremptory woman could have useful information. Perhaps critically important information. Kate said to Taylor, "I'll meet you down at the car."

"You will not. I want him nowhere near these premises."

Kate shrugged acquiescence. "I'll call in when I'm ready."

His hands at the waist of his kelly-green jacket, Taylor adjusted the gunbelt underneath. He flicked a glance at the woman, nodded somberly to Kate, turned away. Kate knew he would remain nearby, in direct radio communication with the C.O. regarding this complication.

Watching him plod down the flagstone path to the cement stairs, the woman said to Kate, "A policeman I can understand — men are domesticated animals at best. Why have you allied yourself with such gun-toting creatures?"

"At times I wonder myself," Kate said.

The woman's swift smile was brilliant — all the more for its unexpectedness. "Perhaps one day you'll closely examine the question."

Kate pulled out her notebook. "Who are you?"

"Put that book away. I refuse to speak if I'm to be recorded." As Kate obeyed, she said, "My name is Gillian Smythe."

Kate knew she had revealed her recognition of the name. Gillian Anne Smythe, married to Martin Brooks Smythe; they had fled to England in 1952.

What was this woman doing here now? Was she hiding Dorothy Brennan? A prickling between her shoulders, Kate stole a glance at the house. She asked, "How long have you lived here?"

"Two and a half months. I tried to return from England when Mother Smythe — my mother-in-law — died nine months ago. I am exactly as you see, Detective Delafield, a seventy-two-year-old woman with more than a touch of arthritis. Do I seem dangerous to you?"

Kate answered as she was expected to. "No."

"Your country required six months to make that decision. When my flight landed I was questioned for hours by two INS goons evidently convinced I would immediately lead a Communist insurrection. I can scarcely wait to depart your land of free speech and free assembly."

If the words were bitter, the face was composed. Kate asked, "Why are you here now?"

"To liquidate my mother-in-law's property. My sister-in-law dropped everything in my lap. I've sold the house; it's in escrow."

"What's your relationship to Meaghan Dorothea Smythe?"

"She's the sister-in-law. Wife of my husband's brother."

"I see. And how long is it since you've seen her?"

Gillian Smythe gestured to a burlap sack covered with plant cuttings. "I have gardening to finish. Perhaps you could assist while I'm answering your questions."

Reminded of Aimee's non-questions that were phrased as questions, Kate smiled. "Whatever I can do." Dirt stains on her pants would be a small enough price. "Are you here alone, Mrs. Smythe?"

"Please call me Gillian. Of course I'm alone; who else would there be?"

"I'll just put my jacket over there," Kate said, indicating a roofed patio at the side of the house. This would give her an opportunity to assess her surroundings.

The beige stucco house, separated from its

251

neighbors by high hedges and citrus trees, was dark and quiet — no sound of a radio or TV. She peered through the glass patio door, saw only shadowy furniture. Watching Gillian Smythe, who was again at work on her weeding, she removed her jacket and unfastened her shoulder holster, placing the jacket, the gun belt underneath, on the patio table; she slid the gun itself into her shoulder bag. She returned to Gillian Smythe, en route picking up an empty burlap sack on which to kneel.

"The daylilies are so badly overgrown — I've divided them, they need transplanting." Gillian was now expertly troweling holes in the flower bed she had weeded and cultivated. "Dorothy always used to be an avid gardener — the flowers have suffered grievously from her inattention."

"How long is it since you've seen her?" Kate asked again. Placing her sack on the grass in front of the flower bed, she knelt, her shoulder bag beside her. The rich smell of freshly turned earth warmed by the sun rose up around her.

"Thirty-six years," Gillian said. "Since nineteen fifty-two."

Kate stared at her. "You haven't seen her at all?"

"Only in photographs. Alistair, and especially Dorothy, never forgave us for leaving. The wound deepened when their daughter Colleen came over to be with us. Martin and I held our family together, you see, while Dorothy's family disintegrated. I gleaned all this from Colleen, and when Mother Smythe visited us, which was often — she was born in England, she and her husband."

Gillian gestured behind her with the trowel. "This was her house, Dorothy lived here with her for years.

When Mother Smythe passed on, Dorothy cashed in her part of the inheritance and simply walked away from everything."

"Walking away from everything seems to be a habit of hers," Kate remarked.

"What is this about two homicides?"

Kate watched her. "We have reason to believe she's responsible."

"Do you indeed. And whom has she supposedly killed?"

"Dudley Kincaid and Owen Charles Sinclair."

"I see." The aged face did not change expression.

"Do you recognize either name?"

Gillian was smoothing the walls of the newly dug holes with the edge of her trowel. "Detective Delafield, we are neither one of us fools. Shall we continue to communicate on that level? I don't know the name Dudley Kincaid."

The woman, Kate noticed, had not donned her gardening gloves. Anne had never gardened with gloves at the house she and Kate had shared in Glendale; she had liked the feel of the earth in her hands. Maybe Aimee would like a house. With a garden like this one. Kate said, "Presumably you're not grief-stricken over Sinclair's death."

"Presumably. Nor Mr. Kincaid's. I presume Dorothy was justified there, as well."

Kate's hackles rose. "Justified?"

"Would you mind?" Gillian Smythe pointed across the flower bed. "I need that sack of treated soil."

Kate rose, and after a moment's hesitation abandoned her shoulder bag. She traversed the flower bed, picked up the sack and carried it back, again kneeling on her burlap bag.

Gillian said, "You surely believe there can be justifiable homicide."

"Two men are dead, Mrs. Smythe —"

"Gillian."

"Gillian." She found it difficult to address this autocratic woman by her first name. "Dorothy Brennan systematically tortured Owen Sinclair —"

"Dorothy Brennan?" Gillian looked up, the pale blue eyes piercing into Kate.

She had said the name inadvertently. "An alias she adopted — apparently after her husband died."

"An alias, you say. We always called her Dorothy — Alistair preferred it to her first name Meaghan. They named their first baby Dorothy. Little Dot, we all called her. Their son's name was Brennan." The blue eyes had clouded, darkened with pain.

Kate said, "I understand your entire family has suffered a great deal."

"Detective Delafield, you don't understand a thing." With a stab of her trowel Gillian Smythe split open the sack and began to shovel the spilling rich dark soil into the holes she had made, filling each one part way.

"Your sister-in-law," Kate said doggedly, "systematically tortured Owen Sinclair with poison over a period of months, then gave him a fatal dose. Over a three-hour period she sat and watched him die the kind of death that belongs in nightmares."

Gillian placed the first cutting in its prepared hollow and handed Kate a spreading fork. "I'll hold the plants in place — will you shovel the untreated earth around them?" The voice was matter-of-fact.

Kate looked into the impassive face, then

obediently forked loam around the cutting Gillian held.

"Back in the forties," Gillian said, "my husband Martin was among the most successful architects in this town. But our great pride was his brother Alistair, Dorothy's husband. Imagine if you can a classical actor with the dramatic intensity of a James Earl Jones, the promise of a young Olivier. Alistair Smythe was an actor so gifted that Chaplin took him under his wing."

"He sounds incredible," Kate offered. Although Gillian Smythe's manner seemed no warmer, her abruptness had altered; she spoke in stately tones, measured phrases.

"Chaplin was convinced Alistair would take a place alongside Olivier, Gielgud, the Barrymores. In nineteen-fifty, Alistair and Martin bought the old Libra Theater on Sunset Boulevard so that Alistair could begin the West Coast equivalent of the Group Theater. Do you know about the Group Theater?"

Kate put aside her gardening tool to spread the warm earth with her hands. "The Group Theater . . ." The name seemed familiar.

"A New York company that revolutionized American drama. Among its members were Harold Clurman, Lee Strasberg, Clifford Odets, Lee J. Cobb, John Garfield . . ." The stately tones became harsh: "And of course Elia Kazan."

Kate remembered Kazan's photo among Sinclair's gallery of informers.

"The previous owner of the Libra Theater had agreed to stage a monstrously bad play Owen Sinclair had written, provided Sinclair put together the financing. I doubt Sinclair could ever have got such a project off the ground, but Alistair made the mistake of contemptuously rejecting it out of hand, refusing to have it defile his new theater. And that's why Sinclair informed on all of us to HUAC. He'd never even laid eyes on any of us except Alistair."

So that was why Owen Sinclair had not recognized Dorothy Brennan . . . Kate watched Gillian press the earth down around the cutting, the knuckles of the liver-spotted hands misshapen with arthritis.

"He was scarcely alone in his perfidy," Gillian continued. "During those times people informed for money, for malice — for reasons having nothing at all to do with politics."

"How did he become so knowledgeable about . . . your politics?" Not even in Vietnam had she encountered any Communists. Gillian Smythe was the first one she had ever met.

"A dinner party. I have no idea how he came to be included. Alistair was there with John Howard Lawson and Lester Cole — you may remember them from the Hollywood Ten. Somehow from that dinner he gathered knowledge about our associations, and all the ammunition he needed."

"I take it Sinclair was the only one who named you?"

"Not at all. But he was first, and that was crucial. The FBI knew about us. With all their surveillance they knew about everyone. McCarthy and his gang uncovered absolutely nothing that the FBI didn't know. But once an informer named you, the FBI and HUAC would use that as leverage on other witnesses, reluctant witnesses, telling them you'd already been named. Some of these witnesses used that as justification. The end result was an accumulation of accusation heaped on those who were named . . ."

Listening intently, Kate continued to fork and smooth earth, working with Gillian Smythe to plant each cutting, the sun hot on her back and shoulders.

"Martin and I were much more politically realistic than Alistair — perhaps because we were older, or perhaps more cynical. Even before the hearings got to Hollywood Martin told Alistair he'd lose his livelihood and his theater. He knew his own business would dwindle to only those souls willing to brave FBI surveillance and harassment. We fled with our two sons while we could still get out somewhat intact."

Gillian rooted the last cutting for Kate to cover with earth. "We pleaded with them to come with us. But Alistair believed profoundly that his future and destiny were here. And Dorothy supported his conviction — she thought it was bound up in his self-confidence, his belief in his talent."

Insects buzzed around Kate, birds twittered and fluttered in the nearby trees. Kneeling on her burlap bag, spreading earth with her bare hands, she felt lulled, hypnotized by her surroundings. "Tell me about Dorothy," she said.

"A woman of extraordinary resourcefulness. In those early years I passionately hated her because she fulfilled the role demanded of women with such intense joy. There was no self-sacrifice in her at all — she worshipped Alistair, she adored her children, she was born to her role of nurturing wife to artistic genius. She's the embodiment of why some very gifted men marry conventionally plain women."

This arresting, articulate woman, Kate thought, was proof of her own statements. She seemed so much more likely to be married to an Alistair Smythe than the prosaic Dorothy Brennan . . .

Gillian started to get to her feet, sat back down. "Would you mind bringing the hose over."

Kate smiled. "Not at all." Another non-question phrased as a question.

Gillian adjusted the trigger nozzle to a fine spray, testing it on the grass. "Then this HUAC business crashed down on our heads."

Carefully, she watered the newly planted bed with short bursts of spray. "Imagine if you can the presence of the FBI in your family's daily life. Two men in a parked car watching your home. A camera set up in a house across the street to photograph visitors to your home. Being followed when you leave your home. Your phones tapped, your mail examined. Your friends, your neighbors, your past and present associates interviewed. Your children isolated because parents refuse to allow their own children to associate with them. Treachery everywhere you turn, the feeling of constantly being hunted — and all because of your beliefs . . ."

The smell of wet earth was intense, dark, fecund. "It's hard to imagine," Kate said, "in a country where it's not supposed to happen." She thought: But being singled out and persecuted is what being gay or lesbian has always been about . . .

"Even from the safety of England it was dreadful to witness a nation assaulting its own best values. We knew that even Martin's trans-Atlantic calls to his mother were tapped. Alistair couldn't work. And the physical safety of his family became such a concern that he got himself a pistol. Little Dot got hold of it . . ." The firm voice quavered.

"We did know about that," Kate murmured.

"She was a tender being who simply could not live in a world where she felt constantly threatened. Her death broke Alistair. His spirit crumbled, his confidence, his self-esteem, his gifts — everything. He began to borrow money — from admirers, friends, his mother. Then came that whole downward slide into the abyss — his infidelities, his drunkenness. Little Dot killed herself on Thanksgiving Day. Colleen told us the holiday seasons afterward were always particularly hideous."

So this was why Dorothy Brennan had destroyed Sinclair on Thanksgiving, and Kincaid on Christmas . . .

"Alistair died an old man at forty-eight, all the life and hope sucked out of him. Their son Brennan was equally self-destructive, he finally found total oblivion in drugs. With all Dorothy's protective, tenacious loving, she could do nothing to prevent two children and a husband from killing themselves, and her last child from fleeing to preserve her own life and sanity. Even from where we were, it was terrible to watch Dorothy's great resilient spirit shrivel away with her agony."

Gillian washed her hands under the hose. "Owen Sinclair smashed all our lives without a qualm, he walked away without a backward glance." She offered the hose to Kate, then wiped her hands on her corduroy pants. "Did you say he took only three hours to die?"

"Gillian." Kate took the hose, turned it on her own hands. "Enough lives have been smashed. It needs to stop. We need to find Dorothy."

"Owen Sinclair destroyed her every reason for existence."

Kate thought: Because Alistair Smythe destroyed Owen Sinclair's last hope for anything. She said, "You wanted to know how I can be a police officer. I do what I can to live in a civilized world. Vengeance isn't my job, or yours, or Dorothy's."

"Isn't it? We're to leave it to God, are we? This country made reparations, however token, to Japanese you interned during World War Two. But people like myself and Martin who were hounded out of our own country, people like Dorothy and Alistair whose lives were utterly destroyed — there never has been any expiation."

"That period in our history is a national shame," Kate said, thinking painfully of Mildred Coates and all her lost possibilities. "It's a matter of national conscience."

"For some, perhaps. Most of you have forgotten. Or think what was done was perfectly appropriate."

"Gillian, Dorothy is no longer fit to judge anything. She's insane."

"Of course she is. Wouldn't you be?"

"Help us find her. Jail seems highly unlikely — an insanity plea is obvious."

"I'm sure. But I don't know where she is."

Kate did not believe her. "Listen to me. This has gone far beyond Owen Sinclair and what he did to all of you. She killed Dudley Kincaid for his politics — simply because he agreed with Sinclair. Her victims have ceased to be people. They're symbols."

Gillian said quietly, "All my life I've been a symbol. My philosophical belief in the simple decencies of equality, dignity and brotherhood have made me a symbol. People who fear other people always turn them into symbols. Killing a symbol is so much easier than killing a person."

Kate's mind filled with the image of Dorothy Brennan's dark glittering eyes, her feral face. "Your sister-in-law is a serial killer. She has a hunger, an appetite for killing. She —"

The beeper in Kate's shoulder bag sounded. She stood, hooking the purse over her shoulder. "I need to call in immediately," she said, adding, "or you'll have police storming up here to find out why I haven't."

Gillian waved her to the house. "Spare me your storm troopers. You may use the phone in the kitchen."

Kate stood in the kitchen with her back against the refrigerator, one hand holding the wall phone receiver, the other around the gun in her shoulder bag. Even if Dorothy Brennan was not now in this house, Kate could feel her brooding, seething presence.

"Kate, is everything all right there?" asked Sandy Berenson, the Detectives Commanding Officer. "Ed has very bad vibes. We have officers deployed on Hyperion."

Touched by Taylor's overreaction, buoyed by Berenson's easy, laconic tones, Kate felt some of her tension ease. The police family was gathered around her. She said, "So far there's no problem, sir. I doubt the suspect is on the premises, but I'm not entirely certain of the situation."

She could picture Berenson's large frame filling a desk chair turned sideways, his feet up on a pulled-out desk drawer, his arms crossed, the phone resting on his beefy shoulder. She said, "Tell Ed the woman he met is Gillian Smythe, and we need a search warrant."

She now understood Gillian's hostility to Taylor — he was too reminiscent of plainclothes FBI men with their badges and guns. "I need more time here," she said. "I should be ready to report in perhaps twenty minutes or so."

"If we haven't heard from you by then . . ."

"Yes sir. I appreciate it."

The kitchen was neat and clean, the living room dark and quiet, its furniture draped with dustcovers. Her hand still on the gun, Kate moved cautiously toward the door. From what she now knew and sensed about Dorothy Brennan, even a .38 Smith & Wesson seemed somehow inadequate.

Gillian Smythe sat on the doorstep with hose in hand, its soft spray raining on another of the flower beds. Kate sat down beside her, her body angled so that she could see the door of the house, the windows. She said, gesturing to the house, "You said she simply walked away. Does she still have personal possessions in there?"

"A great many books of all varieties." Gillian added with distaste, "There was also a vast assortment of conservative periodicals, which I threw out."

Kate remembered *The National Review* on Dorothy Brennan's coffee table the first time she and Taylor had interviewed her. Dorothy Brennan, who started arguments about politics but offered no opinions of her own . . . Why would she be reading conservative periodicals? *Urgent business awaits me,* her note had said.

Chilled, Kate said, "We need to find your sister-in-law."

"Yes, I suppose you do. As I told you, I haven't any idea where she might be."

"No one simply vanishes. We all have networks of acquaintances, the personal habits of a lifetime that leave a trail."

"I doubt you'll find Dorothy quite so predictable. As I also told you, she's enormously resourceful. And she's had thirty-six years to plan and think about this. She has money —"

"How much?"

"Mother Smythe made very good investments. Several hundred thousand dollars I should think."

That would give the cunning Dorothy Brennan far too much flexibility, Kate thought in increasing disquiet. "What about friends? Other relatives? Her own family?"

"I think she has some distant relatives on the east coast — Boston Irish. Her friends? I don't know. Colleen told me their friends were Alistair's friends — some walked away during the trouble, the rest when he died."

Gillian got up, extending the hose to water a far corner. "Do you garden?"

"No," Kate said, welcoming the distraction of the question while her mind worked on the problem of Dorothy Brennan. "Although now I think I'd like to. I'm wondering why you're going to all this trouble over a house you've sold."

"Because the two lovely men who bought it fell in

love with the garden. Like you, I wasn't a gardener when I lived in California, I took the climate, the year-round beauty for granted. But now I've become another of the garden-loving English."

She moved out over the grass and Kate rose to accompany her. Gillian said, "It was quite amazing to find the garden fairly much unchanged from when I used to visit Mother Smythe thirty-six years ago. Over here are the same bearded iris — I transplanted a good many last week, the poor crowded bulbs had pushed out of the ground. And here are the same delphinium, the spectacular ginger lilies. And the verbena — it flowers so beautifully all summer long." Gillian's voice changed, softened: "And here . . . right here is the same patch of English lavender."

Kate's gaze settled on gray-green spikes several feet high near the front of the garden, the leaves narrow and woolly gray-green. Gillian said, "Did you know that in America English lavender only grows here on the West Coast? When I left, it was late spring, the lavender was in full bloom — lovely clusters of deep blue-violet flowers. I dried some — they make quite wonderful sachets — and took them with me. The fragrance lasted for years, believe it or not. For years and years I could smell this lavender . . ."

Kate asked softly, "Did you never want to come back?"

"I have no country to come back to," Gillian said evenly. "Martin considered it, during the sixties. It appeared things were changing. But then Martin passed away. And you elected Richard Nixon, one of the hoodlums who presided over HUAC. Did you know Ronald Reagan was a stool pigeon for the FBI during the days of HUAC?"

"No," Kate said, "I didn't."

"It was in your press — I see the American papers. But nothing at all was made of it. And now you've elected George Bush, who ran your KGB."

Kate shook her head. "Gillian, the CIA is not the KGB."

"The naivete of Americans would be charming," Gillian said, "if it were not so lethal."

Kate asked, "When do you leave the United States?"

"When escrow closes in two more weeks."

"We need two things of you. Your permission to search this house, and a signed statement of what you've just told me about Dorothy in relation to the murders."

Gillian Smythe turned her back on Kate. "Absolutely not."

"We'll obtain a search warrant." And the house would be watched until Gillian Smythe left, and perhaps for a time after that.

Gillian turned around to Kate, looked at her for a moment, then closed her eyes. "Am I to have no surcease from your police state?"

Kate said gently, "This particular police state can't force you to give us a statement. But I'd like you to reconsider your decision. I can't believe you're as unconcerned as you seem about what she may do."

Gillian turned off the hose, shook the remaining drops from the nozzle. "As you sow . . ." she murmured. "I know Dorothy. Clever as you may be, Detective Delafield, it will be extremely difficult for you to find her. I will return to England imagining Dorothy loose like a rabid virus, venting her rage somewhere amid your ultra-conservative right wing. I suppose during all these years I have become as insane in my own way as Dorothy."

"Gillian — why did you talk to me at all?"

Gillian smiled, again that brief, brilliant smile. "Why did I transplant the perennials?"

Kate looked at her in a mixture of profound defeat and profound compassion. "I hope you're at least finding some peace with your family in England."

"I am — to a degree. England is a troubled country in these days of Margaret Thatcher. But it has history and culture. And," Gillian Smythe said, "compared to a newer country which has given so many people so much hope, its mistakes seem much more forgivable."

New Year's Eve

Emerging from the second floor staircase of the Beverly Malibu, Kate halted as she glimpsed Maxine Marlowe. The actress, wearing a red-sequined top over a black skirt, was swaying down the hallway on spike heels toward what had been Lorraine Rothberg's apartment; she carried a silver-handled tray draped with a large cloth napkin. "It's me, boys," she called, and was awarded immediate entrance.

Kate knew that two young men with AIDS had moved into the Rothberg apartment; two more would be occupying apartment 13 as soon as it was repainted and recarpeted. Apartment 13 — where Owen Sinclair's death thirty-seven days ago, and his actions thirty-six years ago, had set in motion a sequence of events still being played out.

Kate rang Paula Grant's doorbell. To her surprise, Houston answered.

"Just leaving," he said, smiling. "I heard the news. The whole building's in a dither."

"We were lucky. How are you?" she asked.

"Quite well, thank you. And you?"

He looked well, she thought as she answered his query. He seemed to have gained a few pounds. She gazed at him in admiration; his flowing white shirt enhanced the taut, dark beauty of his face.

"I'm staying over with Cyril," he said, "to watch the football games tomorrow with the fellows down the hall."

"Houston the sports lover," she teased.

He said with a mock sigh, "Another wasted day of watching gorgeous men in tight uniforms. Happy New Year to you."

"And the same to you," she said, fervently meaning her wish.

"My dear," Paula greeted Kate in her low husky tones. "I'm so glad to see you. Happy New Year." She touched her cheek to Kate's.

Kate murmured her own greeting, wondering if she would ever overcome her feeling of clumsy shyness around Paula Grant.

Aimee lay on the carpet propped on her elbows, the back pockets of her jeans emphasizing the full swell of her hips. She was leafing through a book.

Looking around at Kate through a curtain of dark hair, she smiled and sat up.

Kate felt the familiar rush of pulse at the sight of her. The fresh shock at her beauty. She knelt to embrace her, savoring the welcome of her arms, the faint scent of her perfume, the too brief sweetness of her kiss. "I wanted to be here much sooner," Kate whispered against the silk of her hair.

"I know." Aimee released her, ran caressing fingers down her cheek. "You've had such a rough week."

"Kate dear, would you like something to drink?" Paula asked. "Some wine?"

"Thank you, no." She sat on the floor beside Aimee. What she wanted was to leave, to go home and surrender her tired body and soul to Aimee's arms.

Paula sat down on the sofa and gestured to the TV which was tuned to CNN, the sound turned low. "The story's been on every news broadcast."

If I'd been smarter sooner, Kate rebuked herself for the thousandth time, the story would have ended right here in the Beverly Malibu. "I'm glad we got her before . . ."

She trailed off wearily. She had been on edge all week — Taylor no less than she — working at a frenzied pace, fearing that Gillian Smythe had been right, that the calculating Dorothy Brennan would kill again — perhaps even a number of times — before they could apprehend her.

Aimee said, "Did she actually get close to Nixon?"

"No," Kate said. "Because she gave us some clues

to work with. The pattern of when she killed, the type of victim we knew she'd choose. We felt certain she'd act on New Year's Eve or New Year's Day. And she didn't know that we'd learned who she was."

She closed her eyes, arching under Aimee's hands, the gentle fingers massaging her shoulders. "Nixon's Secret Service men were notified — along with every other conservative politician and right wing individual or organization our task force could conceivably connect with her."

"I told you," Aimee said to her aunt. "It's why this woman's been working twenty-five hours a day all week."

Paula said, "We heard she was disguised as a nurse."

Kate nodded. "And wore a wig."

The Secret Service, on full alert, had surprised, subdued, and arrested Dorothy Brennan without incident nearby the New Jersey home of the former president, confiscating the medical bag she carried: it had contained enough plastic explosive to significantly rearrange a good portion of that very posh Bergen County neighborhood.

We were lucky, she had said to Houston. And indeed they had been. If Dorothy Brennan's insanity had not pushed her this quickly to so prominent a target, she could have killed any number of Owen Sinclairs and Dudley Kincaids. But going after Richard Nixon . . . the Secret Service would grab anything that moved inside their perimeter.

Paula said, "How on earth could Dorothy get her hands on such powerful explosives?"

"I'm sure the FBI will find out. But believe me, Paula, in this country if you have money — and she did — you can get anything. My guess is, she made the buy from one of those right wing survivalist groups."

"How perfectly ironic," Paula murmured. "I suppose a mental hospital is next?"

"I think so," Kate said. "Eventually."

Paula lit a cigarette, then sighed. "I wonder if our own lives will ever return to normal."

"Normal, maybe," Aimee said. "But the same? I know what Dorothy Brennan did, I saw it. But what happened to her and everybody she loved . . ."

She picked up the book she had been reading — *Scoundrel Time,* the Lillian Hellman memoir of the McCarthy years that Paula had given her for Christmas. "Listen," she commanded. "*Listen* to the last lines in this book:

'I am angrier now than I hope I will ever be again; more disturbed now than when it all took place. I tried to avoid, when I wrote this book, what is called a moral stand. I'd like to take that stand now. I never want to live again to watch people turn into liars and cowards, and others into frightened, silent collaborators. And to hell with the fancy reasons they give for what they did.'"

Aimee looked into Kate's face for response.

Silenced by the raw force of the words, by her visions of Dorothy Brennan, Gillian Smythe, and Mildred Coates, Kate nodded.

Aimee turned to her aunt, who sat sipping wine, watching her. "You actually *knew* Lillian Hellman."

"Yes," Paula said, "and I'm glad that finally

you're as impressed with the fact as you should be. You finally understand."

Aimee murmured, "To be tested like that, to put all your integrity on the line . . ."

"We're given tests of our integrity every day of our lives," Paula said. "To prepare us for when the great test comes."

Kate thought: What will I do when I'm given such a test?

Wanting, needing, to change the subject, she said, "I saw Maxine Marlowe in the hallway carrying a tray."

Paula picked up her cigarette. "Bringing some treats to Tommy and Hernando. We all take turns waiting on the boys — this is Maxine's night. She gets gussied up in all her finery, sweeps in there and tells them story after story of her glory days in Hollywood. They love her, I suspect she's their favorite of all of us."

"What all of you are doing is wonderful," Kate said.

"It won't be wonderful when we lose one of them." Grimacing, Paula stubbed out her cigarette. "And oh God, Kate, they *are* boys, they are *so* young . . . And we've got other problems now. The neighbors have gotten wind of what's going on here, they're raising objections."

Paula spread her hands, shrugged. "But I suspect we'll at least win that one. Hazel's waded into battle like Joan of Arc. Taking them on is ever so much more soul-satisfying than fighting the rent control board."

Smiling, Kate shook her head. She turned to Aimee. "Ready to go?"

"Why don't you come over for New Year's tomorrow, the two of you?" asked Paula. "Stay over tonight in the spare room if you like."

No way, Kate thought, trying to compose an articulate objection, there was no way she could go to bed with Aimee in this apartment.

"No way," Aimee said, getting to her feet. "All week I've hardly seen this woman. We're ringing in the New Year in bed, we're spending all day tomorrow in bed." She strode down the hallway, toward the bathroom.

Into the awkward silence Paula said, "Ah, youth."

Staring at the floor, Kate muttered, "She's . . . a bit like being on a raft in white water."

"I was very concerned and upset about this relationship at first," Paula said.

Kate looked at her.

"Attracting women has been all too easy for her, she's used her beauty to cut down women like a scythe. I didn't want you to be one of them. I'm too fond of you. I would hate to lose a chance for a new friendship over the misdeeds of my niece. But this seems quite different — I've never seen her this happy. You're the first woman she's been with that she admires. At this point, my hope is that you won't hurt *her*."

Trying to digest all of Paula's words, Kate said, "I don't intend to."

"We never do," Paula said as Aimee opened the bathroom door and came down the hallway.

She picked up the jacket sweater Kate had given her for Christmas, draped it over her shoulders. "Ready, lover?"

* * * * *

In the car, as Kate turned the key in the ignition the radio came on: the opening chords of *Will You Still Love Me Tomorrow?*

Drumming the beat on the dashboard, Aimee hummed the tune.

"You know the song," Kate said, amazed.

"Sure. You think I was born yesterday?" She ran fingertips over Kate's thigh. "If I can time it right, there's something I'll be doing with you just as our first new year together begins."

Aimee's face was pale and dark sculpture in the shadows of the street. Soon, Kate thought. In the shadows of their bedroom, the gift of beauty that Aimee had brought to her would be hers to possess. Aimee's face would be in her hands . . .

Unbidden, another face edged into her mind. The proud, regal countenance of Gillian Smythe. In another week she would once more journey into exile . . .

"Aimee," Kate said, "I wish I could tell you what it means to have you with me tonight. Before we go home, I need to take you somewhere special to me — for just a few minutes." Thinking about Maggie Schaeffer and the women of the Nightwood Bar, she smiled. "I might even be able to arrange a special version of *Will You Still Love Me Tomorrow?*"

"No kidding. Where are we going?"

Kate pulled away from the curb. "To meet some of my family."

Author's Note

Gratitude is inadequate, but all I can offer to Montserrat Fontes, who brought crucial understanding by revealing the never-healed wounds of a family shattered by the historical events alluded to in this novel.

I am indebted to certain primary research sources. First and foremost, Victor Navasky's brilliant and appalling *Naming Names* (The Viking Press, 1980). Also *City of Nets* by Otto Friedrich (Harper and Row, 1986); *The Celluloid Closet* by Vito Russo (St. Martin's Press, 1987); *Women and the Cinema* by Karyn Kay and Gerald Peary (Dutton, 1977); *The Role of the Script Supervisor in Film and Television* by Shirley Ulmer and C. R. Sevilla (Hastings House, 1986); *Citizen Cohn* by Nicholas Von Hoffman (Doubleday, 1988); *Timebends* by Arthur Miller (Grove, 1987); *Hollywood Red* by Lester Cole (Ramparts, 1981); *Kazan: A Life* by Elia Kazan (Knopf, 1988).

And, of course, *Scoundrel Time* (Little, Brown, 1976) and all the work of the inestimable Lillian Hellman, whose moral voice spoke to her generation and continues to speak to ours.